APPALACHIAN ROOTS
REVISITED . . .

Appalachian Roots Revisited ...

And Maneuvering Life's Briar Patch Beyond

Plus extra bonus chapter of Mama King's Appalachian recipes

NINA STACY THOMAS

Mountain Arbor
Press

Alpharetta, GA

ISBN: 978-1-63183-501-8 - Paperback

Printed in the United States of America   1 2 1 2 1 8

♾This paper meets the requirements of ANSI/NISO Z39.48-1992 (Permanence of Paper)

Cover photo by Jan Daugherty Copeland

For Eric and Ethan.

And in memory of the strong women who raised me,
Mother and Mama King
(Virginia King Wallen and Ruby Barlow King).

I've been absolutely terrified every moment of my life—and I've never let it keep me from doing a single thing I wanted to do.
—Georgia O'Keeffe

I believe writing your own story is redemptive; it makes us practice empathy. I think empathy makes us live more kindly and gently in this hard world.
—Joshilyn Jackson

Contents

Foreword

I was surprised when Nina asked me to write a foreword to her memoir, since I was still the notorious former husband. Although we maintained fairly close contact over the years, the focus of our relationship was always on our son, Eric, the only child of our fifteen-year marriage. Later Eric gave us our only grandchild, Ethan, whom we both cherish.

When looking back on our marriage, it is important that the reader keep in mind the fragility of memory. We are often selective in our memories and usually remember what we want to remember, especially memories that cast us in a good light or serve some useful purpose. I am as guilty of this as anybody. That said, I may see our marriage in a much different light than Nina, although we probably agree on many things. Having just turned eighty, I like to believe that age and maturity helped me overcome the problems that contributed to my share of the blame for the failure of our marriage, but in reality I made great strides prior to the divorce.

On a warm, sunny morning in May sometime in the midseventies, I went to the track at Avondale High School with a young colleague of mine and began a running career that continues today, albeit at a much slower pace. I also eliminated meat from my diet and, most importantly, stopped drinking alcoholic beverages. This did not necessarily mean I was a different person, but did my lifestyle ever change. The reason I disclose this information is to say that I spent four to five years with Nina as somewhat of a "health fanatic," an approach I continue to this day. In revisiting these years of our marriage, I realize that Nina played a significant role in my academic and personal development.

We met in Knoxville while I was completing my undergraduate degree in political science. In June 1964, we walked to the Methodist church, where we were married between the services. Returning to our apartment on Hill Street, we held a reception with a Beatles cover band led by my best man and going high volume. The sixties were in full swing, and Nina and I were always present. In January we left Knoxville for Southern California, where we were soon joined by Eric, the single most important outcome of our marriage, something on which we both agree. Then we returned to Knoxville, where we took a master's degree in political science and Nina found work as a layout ad artist on the University of Tennessee newspaper, the *Daily Beacon*. I was slowly discovering that I was married to someone with a vast array of talents, especially artistic, a talent that both Eric and Ethan inherited from her in abundance.

After Knoxville it was on to Tucson, where we took a PhD in political science from the University of Arizona. These were heady and exciting times and very hard to leave, especially to return to the South, but a job beckoned at Georgia State University, and off we went to Atlanta, where both Nina and I would spend the rest of our lives mostly connected to GSU.

It is fair to say that much of our married life was one great adventure, much of which this memoir is about, but it should be pointed out that although I was most often the impetus for all the movement, never once did Nina complain or fail to cooperate. We may see some things differently, like why we originally went to California and returned, but again, she agreed to the moves. I say this to ensure everyone that Nina was never anything but an agreeable mate. Not only was she cooperative, but she was (and is) interesting. Originally I was attracted by her phenomenal beauty, then she turned out to be one helluva talented person. Our marriage may have ended on the rocks, but it was always interesting.

—William R. Thomas Jr., PhD
Retired Professor of Political Science, Georgia State University
Author, *The Burger Court and Civil Liberties*

Introduction

I've started this memoir numerous times over the years, and until recently I had no idea how to start or end it. But as I've delved into writing, I've become both more surprised at my life and more unsure how to proceed. I suppose I should warn you that I've done nothing as earth-shattering as finding the cure for cancer, nor as impressive as the women mathematicians who helped get astronauts into orbit. So don't expect anything quite as dramatic as that, but it's been an interesting journey that started in Appalachia.

It's definitely complicated and scary to write about your own life. I find myself remembering things that I might not want to remember, or even admit, but I've been forced to either face those things or forget the whole project. So I have made an effort to dig through a foggy memory and reveal as much truth as possible. (Thankfully, I've kept records, journals, and old letters to help.) I've come to think of that as the point of the memoir, and maybe of life. I've found it equal parts healing and re-wounding, but needed for self-recognition and the truth as I remember it.

Recently, I've read some books and articles about memoir writing. One, "Secrets and Lies," starts, "Many first-time memoirists are motivated by self-serving desires: to make the world notice them or to make the world like them" (*Newsweek*, August 9, 2010). That's probably true. The reason I was even reading this old magazine was that it had Mark Twain on the cover and the headline read, "Secrets and Lies, and the American Writer. Twain on Twain, an exclusive excerpt from his complete autobiography." Why would Twain capture my interest? I've always bragged that my birthday, November 30, is the same as Twain's and Winston Churchill's. Good company, wouldn't you agree? It seemed something to brag about until I read more about Twain and found that, although he was loved by most of the world during his lifetime, he might not have been quite so lovable in his personal life. A complicated person, for sure, but aren't we all when it comes down to it?

Okay, why did I have a magazine from 2010 that I'd obviously never read? Well, among other things, apparently I'm both a procrastinator and a book hoarder. I've had the first volume of Twain's autobiography for about five years now and I've never read it, but in my defense it must weigh ten pounds and will take quite a while to read once started—which may or may not ever happen. It's not one I can carry around with me as I usually do with a book I'm in the process of reading. Twain stipulated that his autobiography not be published until one hundred years after his death. I won't make any such stipulation. I hope that my son and grandson might enjoy reading it at some point in their lives. Now that it's too late, I wish I'd asked my grandparents more questions about their lives and recorded their answers.

As Socrates said: "An unexamined life is not worth living." So here goes!

Chapter One
My Mother, the King Family, and My Childhood

Picture an unpretentious white clapboard house in a small town in Virginia, a front porch with rocking chairs and a swing. I whiled away many summer days on that porch with the requisite glass of sweet tea, which, of course, is a "Southern thing." My Granddaddy (Murphy) King or other family members often sat in one or more of the rockers, along with me on the swing, watching the world go by.

On the back porch (off the kitchen) sat a wringer washing machine near a small table and chairs where my grandmother, whom I called "Mama," or other women of the house sat peeling potatoes or stringing green beans. Sometimes a hired woman named Frances ironed clothes there, because it was cooler than inside (before air-conditioning was prevalent).

This house was built by my great-grandfather George Washington Barlow, Mama King's father. I was raised there within an extended family that consisted of my grandparents, Mama and Granddaddy King (Ruby Barlow King and Murphy King); my mother, Virginia Lou (Jenny Lou); and my brother, Jack King Stacy. At times other family members either lived there or visited. When my Uncle Fred came home in 1945 from serving in WWII, he and his new wife, Haline, stayed there until they found a house of their own a few miles away.

Uncle Fred looked much like Mama with his dark and handsome good looks. As Mama's only and adored son, he did whatever he could to help, including mowing the lawn with a push mower, not an easy task on a hilly lawn. Mama and Granddaddy had four children: Virginia (my mother), Marilyn, Fred, and Peggy, in that order. Growing up in our family was like a loving, warm hug every

1

day. Mama was pure love packed in a tiny five-foot-two body with olive skin, brown eyes, and black hair sprinkled with grey. Grand-daddy was just the opposite in looks. He was six feet tall with crystal-clear blue eyes that twinkled when he teased me. I don't remember his handsome self before his hair was white.

The setting was smack dab in the middle of Appalachia in the foothills of the Cumberland Mountain range. It is almost impossible to describe the beauty of living in Pennington Gap, Virginia. I awoke on most days to a misty morning with a dreamlike fog that lifted later to bright sunlight with a blue-green background of hills and mountains. (As shown in the cover photo.)

The main street, Morgan Avenue, is considered to be on the Trail of the Lonesome Pine, named after a book by that title written in 1908 by John Fox Jr., who lived in Wise County next door to my Lee County. A drama with that name plays each summer a few miles away in Big Stone Gap, Virginia, with all the actors being local folks. It is reported to be the longest-running outdoor drama in the United States and is the "official outdoor drama" of the Commonwealth of Virginia.

The play centers around the love story of a couple caught in a thirty-year feud between their two mountain families. Though the love story sounds familiar (Romeo and Juliet?), the drama involves coal mining versus industrialization of the region at the turn of the century. The plot is appropriate, because coal mining was the main industry of the area for many years. The more recent novel *Big Stone Gap* is yet another adaptation based on the region, and its characters live in a coal-mining community. Author Adriana Trigiani also wrote and directed the 2015 movie of the same name, but she added some comic relief in her story. Growing up, I knew some of the real-life characters in the book, though their names were changed.

The Trail of the Lonesome Pine is also called "Wilderness Road," which is the trail Daniel Boone blazed to find a route through Virginia to the Cumberland Gap in central Kentucky and beyond. A reconstructed fort at Martin's Station in Lee County's Wilderness Road State Park on the route to Cumberland Gap relates some of the long history of Boone's journey.

Because of this trail, many Scots-Irish, English, and German immigrants came and settled in the Carolinas and Virginia. Many stayed in the winter of the late 1700s, because the weather was so cold that they were forced to settle there rather than continue their journey. From them came the Appalachian dialect that the Southerners of that area inherited and continue to use, derived from Elizabethan English as well as Irish and Scottish words, songs, and stories.

I've observed many people from the region move away and intentionally change their accent. No matter how many places I've lived since (that includes five states in all), I have never tried to rid myself of my Southern accent, because I'm proud of my heritage.

Back to my family, whom I adored. My mother was known to friends and family as Jenny Lou. To say that Mother was secretive about things she found sensitive is an understatement. Apparently, she opted to change her middle name to suit herself. Instead of the middle name of Louisa, which she was given by her parents, she always used the middle name Lou. I didn't find this out until after her death. I also didn't realize how much I loved and would miss her until 2014, when she passed away at ninety-five years old. She was divorced from my father, Jack Kirk Stacy (for reasons I learned later). It was a time when divorce was not common. She had to work throughout my youth, as an x-ray technician at Lee General Hospital. From information I've learned about him, I am grateful that I had the upbringing I did rather than ever living with my father. I will eventually get to the devastation my mother suffered due to his mistreatment, but for now I'll discuss more cheerful family matters.

I've heard of families who haven't seen or kept in touch with relatives for years, but with the exception of an estrangement from my father, I can't imagine that fate. I am thankful for our family rituals. For instance, we had a feast each Sunday after church. We didn't call it a feast, but it was always a delicious meal prepared by Mama King and any other female relatives who happened to be around. Mama and Mother and daughter Peggy, or daughter-in-law

Haline, would have the meal ready around noon when church was over at the First Baptist Church. I've no idea how they managed to attend Sunday school and church and have everything ready; they must have taken turns. We were a churchgoing family, so it never occurred to me to question or attempt not attending every time the church doors were open. The cover photo of this book shows that church, and our house (gone now) was only a block away.

Family gatherings around the table on Sundays are some of my fondest memories. Meals at Mama King's were always good, but the Sunday meal was special: the table was always set in the dining room with a linen tablecloth, cloth napkins, fine china, and Mama's good cooking. In summer, roses appeared on the table cut from Mama's heirloom light-pink rosebush in the backyard.

Any immediate family members living in town were always there, and of course any out-of-towners. When Granddaddy's sisters and their families were in town, it was a happy, loud celebration. All five of his sisters—my Great-Aunts Verda, Bess, Ada, Vera, and Eva—each lived to reach their hundredth year, or each well into her nineties. In fact, along with a party thrown by the family for her, Verda's one hundredth was covered in her local news, the *Lexington Herald-Leader* (June 29, 1999). (Granddaddy Murphy and his brothers, Smith and Roy, did not have the same luck with longevity.) The sisters were all college-educated teachers. Some were schoolteachers, others music or art teachers, but all were talented at their specific calling. They were the most cheerful people I've ever encountered. They talked and talked over each other, laughing and claiming they could hear each other and express themselves at the same time. I tend to believe it was true. It was a happy, happy time. As is often the case, I didn't appreciate it then, yet it is something I now cherish and miss.

As I mentioned, Granddaddy and his brothers did not live as long as their sisters, but still they left stories for me to tell. Granddaddy's seventy-eight-year-old brother, Roy (a merchant), and his seventy-seven-year-old wife, Vera, both died on the same day, which to me seems like a very romantic, if sad, ending to their lives.

Vera had gone to church earlier than Roy, but when he did not show up as planned, she went to check. When Vera arrived home, she found the body of her husband and, according to authorities (quoted in newspaper articles), she suffered a heart attack on the street as she was frantically running to get help. They were both pronounced dead on arrival at the hospital.

Another brother of Granddaddy, Findley "Smith" King, was married twice; the reason being that he accidently shot his first wife, Ollie Mae. They were very young (he thirty-two and she twenty-eight) and had three young sons: Herb, Hugh, and Edwin. Here is an account of the incident quoted from a (obviously) small-town newspaper (I'm not sure what newspaper the clipping is from, c. 1922).

> *On last Saturday night, after mid-night, Mrs. Smith King was for some reason, at the window of her bed room [sic], when her husband was quickly aroused from sleep, and supposing it to be a burglar at the window, quickly drew his pistol from under his pillow and fired in the direction of the noise. The screams of his wife told him plainly that he had shot his wife. The bedroom was an upper chamber and the window was over the porch roof, which Mrs. King fell out of when shot and rolled off the porch roof onto the ground, a distance of about 12 feet. Mr. King ran to the yard where her body had fallen lifeless from the roof. Then the grief strickened [sic] man began to call to her to answer him but no answer came. The alarm soon spread, and neighbors gathered to the scene, but found Mrs. King was dead. E. P. Steward, Coroner, called a jury and held an inquest, as required by law. After a preliminary hearing the jury decided it was an accidental shot that killed Mrs. King.*

An interesting aside to the above story is that I belong to Ancestry.com and had them do my DNA, which is posted online. Recently I was notified of a DNA match with a possible fourth cousin, who wanted to contact me. It turned out to be a relative I'd met

(Dennis King) years ago at a family reunion but, due to distance, hadn't kept in touch. Due to the Ancestry DNA match, we have since talked and shared family stories and information and hope to continue a kin relationship, if only by phone. He is the son of Hugh King, one of the three sons of Smith and Ollie Mae King (of the story above). So thanks, cousin Dennis, for reminding me of this family story. How cool is that?

Granddaddy's father, E. R. King, was also a merchant. He owned and operated a general store that was called a mercantile store back in the day. He sold all sorts of things, from groceries, dry goods, and tools, and featured a counter in front that enticed the buying of all sorts of candy and goodies. I'm told that the store he owned earlier even sold caskets from the basement. That first store he owned was in a Lee County community called Hagan (near Rose Hill) until his children needed to go to school. There were no schools (for his eight children) in the rural area in which they lived, so he moved his family to Pennington Gap, where he built a large, beautiful, Victorian-style house, much like the one he left in Hagan. His daughter, my Great-Aunt Verda, was an artist and painted pictures of that house, which featured a wraparound front porch. That house is still there but has gone through many structural changes and looks nothing like the original. It's a shame that the lovely and inviting wraparound porch was removed.

The question I wish I could answer about my great-grandfather is one that I cannot. All I know is that he had a leg amputated caused by an accident that involved a train. How or why that happened, I have no clue. All I remember is that my cousin Eddie Carter (Great-Aunt Eva's son) used to take his grandfather's artificial leg and run away with it as a joke. Don't you know that a little boy would find that a fun activity? Well, that little boy, Ed Carter, grew up to work as a news anchor for WIS-TV in Columbia, South Carolina, from which he retired after twenty years in 1998. (See photo of young Ed with his uncle [my granddaddy] and my brother.)

Back to E. R.'s son, my granddaddy. Granddaddy King was a former mayor of my hometown of Pennington Gap, Virginia. The tale here is that when he ran for a second term, his daughter Peggy's father-in-law, J. C. Smith Sr., ran against him and won. Since Aunt Peggy was never at a loss for words, I'm fairly certain that this caused some friction in her household with her husband, J. C. Jr.— for a time anyway.

Granddaddy was remarkable in that he was paralyzed on one side of his body from an auto accident in his thirties or forties; however, being paralyzed did not keep him confined until his later years. He used a cane to walk to church a block away and to town to visit with his buddies at one of the two drugstores, or wherever they gathered to exchange their tall tales. He had been a salesman for the Swift Company when he had the wreck. The story goes that he had a passenger riding with him who got pinned under the car. In order to free the man, he lifted the car off him. Granddaddy was a tall, strong man, but the strain of lifting the car caused a large blood clot on his brain. The clot was removed, but left him paralyzed. Throughout his life, though, I never heard him complain, even years later when he had to have a leg amputated from the knee down and was bedridden.

When I speak of my mother, Virginia King Stacy Wallen (Jenny Lou), I can't find words good enough to describe her. As with most children, I didn't always show her the respect she deserved while alive, and I realize that it is too late to tell her how much I admire the legacy she left for me with her quiet strength and dignity. But at least I can try to tell more of her life than the devastation she suffered from my father. That will come in detail later, but suffice it to say she survived some difficult times. She suffered not only the situation my father put her through, but the loss of her second husband, James Parr Wallen, through his fight with alcoholism (which he eventually won) to his fight with lung cancer, which he lost, and she lived through the worst thing that can happen to a mother: the death of a son, my younger brother, Jack King Stacy. His death was unexpected and heartbreaking to us all. He and his wife, Debbie, raised three wonderful children: Ramey (mother of his beloved granddaughter, Maddy), Chris, and Sarah. After Jack's death, and due to age, Mother was forced to leave the town she'd lived in all her life and move in with me. The woman was never loud, but her strength and determination showed through. It is also unfortunate that my brother didn't live to know the grandchildren born after his death. Chris and wife, Lindsay, have Jackson, named after his grandfather, and Sarah and husband, Alex Wear, gave little Luca Barlow Mama King's maiden name. Jack would adore them as much as he did his beloved Maddy.

As is evidenced in her photos, Mother was a beautiful woman with high cheekbones, a perfectly shaped nose, full lips, and a slender figure. She was fastidious about her appearance. It wasn't because she thought herself a beauty, but just the opposite, because she didn't see herself as such. Her goal was to be neat, clean, and "well put together," and she always was. When she went to work as an x-ray tech, her white uniforms were always starched and ironed and her shoes polished every night to perfection. It was before uniforms were wrinkle free and shoes didn't need polish. She was the same with her children, my brother, Jack, and me. We were sometimes scrubbed raw, but in a good way. Never let it be said that Jenny Lou's children were anything but clean and wrinkle free—at least when they started out for the day.

She was born with red hair so curly that she had ringlets like Shirley Temple when she was a young girl. (See photo.) Later the ringlets were more waves than curls, but still red. Her skin was flawless because she refused to expose it to the sun for fear of the freckles that she hated.

There were times when I thought of Mother as weak, because when confronted she was never loud or confrontational. I now realize that she was very strong in her own way. There was never a loud argument; she just held her ground quietly and firmly. I couldn't have picked a better mother, and I thank God that she spent the last years of her life with me.

When I think of Mother, it might seem odd that I remember spring cleaning, but I do. In the early years, Mama and Granddaddy's house was heated by coal-burning fireplaces and, later, an oil furnace. The mode of heating throughout the winter left a layer of grime on the walls, and the cleaning process fascinated me. The grown women would use a wad of grey, doughy substance to wipe the wallpaper. In fact, when that substance outlived its usefulness as a cleaner for wallpaper, a creative genius named Joe McVicker became a millionaire before his twenty-seventh birthday by finding another use for it. He reintroduced it as the brightly colored Play-Doh that children mold into shapes today. Mother said the substance they used was called "Climax." Odd name, I know, but I'm relying on the memory of a then ninety-year-old woman. All the rooms had wallpaper, and the women—Mama, Mother, Haline, or whoever was around to help—would take a wad of "Climax" and start on the ceilings and go all the way down, rubbing the grime off the walls inch by inch. When that wad was dirty, they would discard it and get another wad to continue wiping. When finished, the wallpaper in each room was as clean as when it was new.

Spring cleaning also included taking slipcovers off the sofa and chairs to be washed and ironed before being returned to the furniture. Windows were washed inside and out, and curtains were washed, starched, and ironed before rehanging.

Adults in the household had to work. Because Granddaddy was disabled, he wasn't able to work in his later years. Mama worked when needed and when work could be found in our small town. She was a sales clerk in a clothing store for a time and later worked in the cafeteria of Pennington High School, where I attended. The school kids (including me) loved her chocolate cake with chocolate icing.

Mother worked as an x-ray technician at the hospital, and because she didn't drive a car until later in life, she walked to work. When she was on call, she walked to and from work at all hours of the night. The town is only three miles long on the main street of Morgan Avenue, but still I'm sure that walking at night, even in those less dangerous days, was not something she enjoyed. Again, my family did not complain about adversity. So I never heard Mother complain.

Uncle Fred didn't live in the household, but he helped his

parents with finances, as did all their children. Fred was a mail carrier long before they had small vehicles to help with the delivery. He walked with a leather pouch on his back from house to house to deliver mail. Needless to say, he did not have a weight problem. Aunt Marilyn, Mother's sister who lived in Cincinnati with her family (husband Murl Rush and daughters Ann and Catherine), worked past her retirement in order to help with Mama's expenses when she was older and unable to work. Their daughter Catherine was crowned Miss Teenage Cincinnati in 1967. She and husband, Tim, hyphenated their last names so that both go by Rush-Ossenbeck. Cool, huh? As for Ann, who is married to internist Dr. David Edelberg, she decided to change her last name to just Raven, thus, Ann Raven came into being later in her life. Don't remember exactly why, but it suits her.

Aunt Marilyn's husband, artist Murl Rush, whom we called Uncle Rush, was art director at WKRC-TV studio in Cincinnati. (See photo.) I'd always assumed it was the studio from which the TV sitcom *WKRP in Cincinnati* came. I've since learned that the sitcom was actually about WQXI-TV in Atlanta. Regardless, WKRC was where my uncle worked, and it was with George Clooney's father, Nick, who was news anchor at the time. I like to think that that makes two degrees of separation between me and George Clooney. I realize that's a pipe dream, but humor me with my fantasy! When Rush retired, Nick Clooney was the MC at his roast.

Growing up in the extended family household held many poignant memories for me, and still does. Mama and I could get tickled and laugh about the same things. Sometimes it would be one of those "church laughing fits" where you couldn't stop laughing, and every time you looked at each other the fit would start again, until tears rolled down your face and your stomach hurt. And of course it was always someplace like church, where we weren't supposed to laugh and people looked at us like we'd lost any sense we ever possessed.

There is one funny story worth sharing that involves Mother and Granddaddy. One night, everyone in the household was gone somewhere, leaving me alone for what I'm sure was a brief period of time. Mother called on the phone to make sure I was okay, and while on the phone with her, I heard Granddaddy trying to get in and the door was locked. I told Mother to hold on while I answered knocking at the door. I knew it was Granddaddy, but apparently didn't think to tell Mother. So I put the phone down and couldn't get the key to work while Granddaddy tried to turn the handle, so I kept yelling "Let go, let go," which was what Mother was apparently hearing. Finally I let Granddaddy in, but when I went back to the phone, Mother was no longer on the line. You can guess what happened . . . A few minutes later I heard a panicked Mother screaming my name while running to the house to make sure I was unharmed.

Not that it relates to this story, but that was the period of time when we had party lines. If someone was using the line you shared, then you had to wait until they were finished with their call before you could use the phone or receive calls. And yes, it would have been possible to listen in on their call if you chose to do so, but no, we didn't. Ah, how times have changed!

Until rereading thoughts about my early life here, I considered myself a fairly normal person from a fairly normal family. That is not to say that I would change a single thing, but I'm not sure any family could be called normal in the eyes of another. I look back at a social anthropology course I took in college, and I think it would confirm the idea that each family is unique. Every family unit is normal to its members, but might not be so-called "normal" in another environment. I also think of a quote by author Ransom Riggs: "I used to dream about escaping my ordinary life, but my life was never ordinary. I had simply failed to notice how extraordinary it was!" Having noted all this, I'm proud to be a part of my family. I'm also proud of the family members who have yet to be introduced, and an interesting bunch they are. So read on and meet other people who were a part of my life, and other experiences. Some were good and some not so good, but all the not-so-good hurdles were jumped and conquered. See how!

Granddaddy King (Murphy) and his brothers and sisters (including sister's married names). From left around the table: Eva (Carter), Roy, Verda (Miller), Smith, Bess (McNeil), Murphy, Ada (Rector), and Vera (Johnston).

JACK, DEBBIE, AND THEIR GRANDCHILDREN

Jack King Stacy (1945–2009)

*Sister-in-law Debbie Miller Stacy
with baby Luca Barlow Wear*

Madelyn (Maddy) DeBusk

Jackson Stacy

Uncle (married to Aunt Marilyn) Murl H. Rush Jr.,
retired art director from WKRC Cincinnati

L–R (King relatives): cousin Catherine Rush-Ossenbeck, niece Sarah Stacy, mother Virginia King Wallen, Nina, and cousin Ann (Rush, Eddelberg) Raven

L–R (King relatives): cousin Ann Raven, cousin Susan Smith Tieche, Nina, cousin Catherine Rush-Ossenbeck, and seated on the floor, niece Sarah Stacy

Mother as a little girl

Mother, Virginia King Stacy Wallen
(1919–2014)

Eric and Mother at nephew Chris's wedding

Mama and Granddaddy King and their children, Ruby Barlow King and Murph King (seated), and children (L–R) Marilyn, Peggy, Fred, and Virginia (Mother) c. 1940s

Granddaddy King

Mama King

Uncle Fred G. King

Granddaddy Murph King (former mayor of Pennington Gap), cousin Ed Carter, who grew up to work as a news anchor for over twenty years at WIS TV station in Columbia, South Carolina, and my brother Jack King Stacy

Chapter Two

School Years

I don't remember that much about grade school, but in both my grade school years and high school years, I went to segregated schools. Judge me if you will, but being a kid, I thought nothing of it. It was just the way things were, and I certainly wasn't one who questioned the status quo. I was too shy to ever be an activist. I saw the African American kids walking to "their" school and didn't question the fairness of it. My family (those within my household) and most friends referred to the black community as "colored." We did not use uglier words in reference to them, though that is not to say that others in town didn't use them. There is a large stone formation overlooking one of the winding roads near the town that is now referred to as "Old Stone Face," but that is not how it was referred to back then. Then it was "N----- Head Rock." Yes, those were the times of my youth that I was too young to question.

There was another group of people who lived in several states in the Appalachian area, who were referred to as Melungeons. Again, I wasn't aware of the mystery or the origin associated with these folks when I was younger. Like most young people, I was self-centered enough to be far more interested in my own issues. Regardless, these folks are a group described as multiracial. Due to the fact that racism was prevalent, I think that the elders of the families kept their origins secret, if they even knew of that origin themselves. It kept them from being assigned to any particular racial group. I went to school with Melungeon kids, never knowing at that time that they were classified as such. Though, again, my memory is vague, I now remember them as good-looking kids who mostly kept to themselves.

There are all sorts of theories about Melungeon origin. The mixtures are thought to come from mixed marriages (in the Southern states mentioned below) among Europeans, Native Americans, African Americans, and maybe even shipwrecked Portuguese sailors. Melungeons tend to have dark complexions, much like people from the Mediterranean area, with European or Anglo features, so it would be difficult to put them into a mold of any kind. Their ancestors are usually traced back to colonial Virginia, Tennessee, Kentucky, and the Carolinas. The fact that they are associated only with this region is why I mention them.

Other theorists think that there were possibly mixed marriages from the Lost Colony. You might remember that in the 1500s a hundred or so English men, women, and children were left on Roanoke Island to establish a permanent settlement in the New World. A few were sent for supplies and, due to a war, were unable to get supplies back to the colony for three years. When they got back, they found the colonists gone. What happened to them is a mystery to this day. One theory is that they were abducted by Native Americans and perhaps married some, bringing a mix of races. Very few people agree on Melungeon origins, and each family would probably need their DNA traced separately to know their true mix.

On the internet, there are lists of surnames of people who might be considered Melungeon. There is no guarantee that those are totally accurate due to the years of secrecy. I've no theory to add, except that from the list of those names most any of us from the area could be considered Melungeon or have relatives within the group. Regardless of our complexion or perceived prejudices, we all fit into the group called the human race, and that should be enough description, except for those more curious about their mix. I, personally, love a good mystery.

On another subject, and don't laugh here, I walked to and from school every day (elementary and high school both). No, it wasn't miles and miles in three feet of snow, but nevertheless it was walking in whatever weather. I'm not sure how long the walk was, but probably a mile or so. In elementary school, I think I might have walked back and forth for lunch at home on occasion, but not every day. However, I do remember one time in first grade, I had a part in a little shadow-puppet show that was to happen right after lunch, and I came back late. The mean ol' teacher punished me by not letting me do my part in the show. I still remember my disappointment and hurt feelings.

In second grade, the teacher believed in using the paddle. I remember it as a wooden thing with holes in it. She paddled us for missing spelling words. I must still hold some resentment, because I can't imagine how that helped with spelling. It might have helped had we learned to spell derogatory words to use toward her, behind her back, and after class, of course. It makes me smile mischievously just to think about doing that.

I've heard it said that if you peak in high school, there isn't anywhere to go from there. I was relieved of that fear because I did not peak in high school—in fact, far from it. Let's just say that I was not a dedicated scholar. As for talent, I did have some innate artistic ability, but that hardly helped where algebra was involved. I found studying boring, and math was the bane of my existence. Looking back, especially where math was concerned, I've often wondered if I had a learning disability that was never diagnosed, but back in those days learning disorders were unknown or unexamined, as far as I know. I accepted being average in scholastics and my artistic talent adequate to overcome at least that one deficit. Sometime during that period, I came to the realization that I was not going to compete with my math-gifted classmates to be valedictorian, but receiving praise and accolades for art projects and fairly good grades for writing assignments were adequate for my self-esteem. As for facing any hurdles in categories where I did not excel, I was smart enough to know where my talent lay and found that determination and persistence worked in my favor.

While on summer break from high school one summer, I took an extension course offered from the University of Virginia. It was a painting course, and the teacher was quite complimentary of me. One painting I remember doing was a copy of a Picasso in his blue period (before cubism) that my cousin Jane ended up with. The instructor told Jane's mother, my Aunt Gladys, in reference to me (and I quote): "She is so talented that it is scary." As you can see, compliments are easily remembered over the years!

In my household, adults were in the process of making a living and dealing with everyday necessities. Future education was not discussed. I was expected to do my homework, but mostly left to do it on my own.

As I mentioned before, I rarely questioned authority, but I think I always knew that I would eventually leave my hometown. I'd figure out the details when the time came. That is not to say I didn't love that town (and still do), but I knew it did not hold my future. Like most girls whose formative years happened in the 1950s, I envisioned getting married and having children, and college factored in there somewhere, if only to enhance my artistic ability.

Boys and a fun social life held my interest. As for boys, I had no idea what a normal interaction was with the male gender. In my household, there was my crippled, bedridden grandfather and sometimes my Uncle Fred, both of whom were stoic at best. They were dear, sweet, and loving men, but not role models with advice for a young girl who was very much in need of it.

My father and mother were divorced when I was five years old. My brother was five years younger, which means that we were of the age difference where we mostly ignored each other or fought on rare occasions. So there you have it with the men in my life, or lack thereof.

My father was in the air force and had another family on the West Coast. When on rare occasions he came to visit his parents (and supposedly my brother and me), he mostly bragged about his newer family and what those children were doing. He didn't seem interested, or at least didn't ask about what was going on with us. I think he was so interested in impressing that it never occurred to him that he was causing emotional harm to my brother and me, but he did manage to do that, one way or another, every time we saw him. There is a whole other tale about him and his antics to come.

As I've analyzed it over the years, I think he was an insecure man who liked to brag about things in his life to his brother and nephews, especially about his womanizing exploits. Of course, they ate it up, and he felt their awe. Whether the awe was earned or not is debatable. Also, I've learned from a source close to him that he suffered brain injuries from several plane crashes during WWII and was paranoid, among other mental health issues. I never knew him well enough to know what was in his mind or heart, but I know he exaggerated and sometimes invented, so I was never sure whether what he was telling me was true.

Some might say that to suggest abandonment by my father would be an exaggeration, but as far as I know, he never contributed financially to my upbringing (or emotional stability) nor that of my brother, so I stand by it as an accurate statement. My mother struggled and did a valiant job of supplying us with all the love possible, as well as all our needs.

Back to boys in my life. My theory is that when I picked a boyfriend, I was trying to find a male who had a reputation much like my father: a self-centered womanizer. Though at the time I didn't have conscious thoughts about it, I suppose I hoped to find and fix my father. Needless to say, it never worked, and many times when a boy would seem to care, I'd find a way to break up with him. Self-preservation, I think that would be called, again with no conscious thought to the emotions. The one man (father figure) in my life basically abandoned me, so I questioned if I was lovable to the male gender. I was trying in my inept way to deal with that. I think I was mostly on the defensive, because my mother's admonition was always "Men—you can't trust them." I know that she meant no harm, but due to her own trauma with my father, she thought she was helping to keep me from being hurt.

This is reminiscent of some information about my father and his military wounds shared by an unnamed source. According to the source, he expected people to reject him, so he just did it first. However, that was much later in his life. The trauma he put my mother and others through in his earlier years is unforgivable and will be told in detail later . . . as I continue to promise.

Now, let me make it clear that everything in my life was not gloom and doom. And even if it had been, I'd have found a way to overcome it as I did with any adversity throughout my life.

Speaking of dealing with adversity, I'm not sure if our high school was large enough for cliques, but there was at least one incident where I was bullied by what today would be called "mean girls." For whatever reason, a rumor was started that I was pregnant. It might have been one of many times when I'd gained some unwanted weight. Weight is yet another issue with which I've dealt on and off most of my life. I tend to be an emotional eater. Up and down go the scales depending on how sad or happy I am. However, the irony of this tale is that not only was I not pregnant, but there was no way I could have been. I was a virgin when I graduated high school. I don't remember who the girls were now, except for one, Brenda, whose last name will be withheld, as there would be no point in naming names after so many years. The only reason I remember her was that she was the driver of the car when they realized the error of their rumor and came by my house to see if I wanted to go hang out with them. Having heard of their deception, my Mama King and mother would not allow me to go with them— that day, anyway. The lesson learned from that experience was that the truth does win out eventually.

From top to bottom: Nina, Mary F. Jessee, Jack Woodard, Carolyn Baker, Sue Yates. I think we were officers of band club. Sue and I got into mischief together.

Nina as a majorette in Pennington High School band c. 1958–1959

Lifelong friends from grade school and high school:
Mary Jessee Tiller and Sue Lawson Buzby

Chapter Three
Minstrel Shows and Other Small-Town Entertainment

In our small town, we used to have minstrel shows. I don't remember much about my younger life, but I do remember that as a preschooler, maybe four or five, I was taught a silly poem to recite for the minstrel audience. "Ooie Gooie was a worm, a noble worm was he. He climbed upon a railroad track, the train he did not see. Ooie Gooie."

I was supposed to repeat the poem sitting on someone's lap, and though I remember rehearsing it, I don't think I was able to recite it when I saw the audience staring at me. Whether this caused my lifelong fear of public speaking, I don't know, but I've always suffered from that affliction.

This annual event was something the population of the town looked forward to. It was the 1940s, the era of radio shows like *Amos 'n' Andy* and others in the same genre. Imagine listening to the radio for entertainment before TV! Now, before I get much further, let me make it clear that I do not mean to imply that racism did not exist or that it was ever okay, then or now. I'll have to admit that it was embedded in the culture of the time, and probably still is to some extent. Small-town rural America in Appalachia could not have escaped it. I can say that hate was not taught in the household in which I grew up, so I did not get the sense that the minstrel show was meant to be mean spirited. Of course, there would have been other options as a venue for entertaining, such as a variety show (without blackface), but that isn't what was chosen. Again, I was young, and whatever the show was, right or wrong, as a youngster I didn't know the difference at the time. For entertainment in a small town, there weren't that many options. There were high school athletic events, a movie theater showing mostly B movies, and every now and then a dance.

In the minstrel shows, the black-faced characters were played by leaders of the white community, people everyone knew and enjoyed a chance to laugh at. My schoolteacher, maiden Aunt Ida, had long dated a local pharmacist referred to as "Doc" Parsons, and the two of them were always mentioned in some humorous way. Hardly anyone escaped being the butt of jokes. They were not offended, but seemed to enjoy a good laugh at their own expense or that of friends.

If it sounds as though I was self-centered and oblivious to discrimination in my youth, that might be true, but (though I don't normally brag about it) I think it important to mention that my adult way of caring is donating to worthy causes. I've worked on at least two Habitat for Humanity projects (when I was physically able) and regularly donate to such charities as the Christian Appalachian Project, Fugees Family (refugees), American Kidney Services, USO, St. Labre Indian School, St. Joseph's Indian School, St. Jude Children's Hospital, and the National WWII Museum, to name a few.

There were two drugstores in town. The drugstore where Doc Parsons ruled was referred to as "the pharmacy," and the other was referred to as the "upper drug." The pharmacy was where folks gathered to socialize. There were booths and a soda fountain. They had a small grill that made the best grilled-cheese sandwiches that I remember to this day.

It was at "the pharmacy" that a nice, grandfatherly man used to slip me dimes on occasion. As in most small towns, everyone knows everyone, and he was a well-known person in the community, a regular at the gathering place with his family.

It would be different today, I'm sure, but in early grade school, when I was about seven to ten, my mother allowed me to go to the movies alone if friends were not available. That meant that I was at the Lee Theater most every Saturday and sometimes on Sunday (after church, of course). Admission was twenty-five cents, and popcorn, candy, and other treats were ten cents.

On a couple of occasions, the grandfatherly man who gave me dimes at the drugstore came to sit beside me when I was alone at the movies. The first time or two, he squeezed my knee and slipped me a welcome dime, which meant an additional candy. I didn't think too much about the knee squeeze, because adults often gave me a pat on the back or a squeeze or hug. Mother had given me treat money, but I was pleased to have the extra dime. However, and I'm sure you know where this is going, on about the third time after he sat beside me and handed me a dime, his hand moved up my leg and he tried to get fingers into my panties. I was both shocked and scared, knowing that was not right, and I bolted from the seat and moved across the theater to another seat. I was scared but knew that I would *never* allow that to happen again. I also knew it was a bad thing to do. Unfortunately, I thought it was my fault because I'd been accepting the dimes, thus I never told my mother or anyone else. Thank God he never tried to bother me again. I'm sure he knew that if such a rumor was spread in a small town, his reputation would have been ruined forever.

But there is a "however" here. I've since heard rumors that yet another supposedly upstanding citizen, a middle-aged man, tried a similar maneuver with one of my girlfriends. (To respect her privacy, I will not use her name here.) These men will not be named, because they've probably both been dead for years, and if they have family still living . . . there's just no point. But the rumor went that this man was a shoe salesperson, and when my friend was trying on shoes, he asked how much she weighed. Why? one might ask. Apparently that was his excuse to lift her by her crotch to check her weight. Of course, weight has nothing to do with buying shoes, but I suppose that pedophiles can come up with all sorts of reasons to get away with their actions. Like me, she never told her mother because she wasn't sure exactly what had happened or how to explain it. Perverts count on that.

Remember the movie *American Graffiti*? Well, that was a good example of what we teens did for entertainment. It was the time of girls with poodle skirts and boys with ducktail-combed hair. We rode around and around with friends and always ended up at our one-and-only drive-in restaurant at some point during the night. If we didn't have a car, we had friends who at least had access to one from parents.

As I mentioned, our small town did not offer a lot in the way of entertainment, so my mother and I were often at the same functions, like dances. Folks of all different ages were eager to attend most any event that offered something other than the drudgery of everyday life.

Although Mother's favorite music was the Big Band Era, she adapted to the times as the music changed. Mother was attractive, a terrific dancer, and a divorcee when I was a teen (she later married her second husband, J. Parr Wallen), and she was sought out for dances even by boys my age. I didn't resent this; it made me proud to have an attractive mother who was a good dancer. By this time it was the era of rock and roll, and like me she learned all the current dances: first the jitterbug, then the shag, continuing with whatever dances were popular.

In the summer, at least once, I worked as a carhop at the drive-in restaurant called Mutt and Jeff's. It was named after the cartoon characters, and I'm pretty sure that no effort was made to legally use the name. Regardless, the names fit perfectly because it was owned by our two high school coaches, Allen Steel (football) and Frank Hensley (basketball). Obviously one was short and the other tall, football and basketball in that order. My friend Sue Lawson (Buzby) and I earned spending money as carhops, and though we didn't do it on roller skates, I remember it as a fun job. (Sue and I stay in touch nowadays via email, and another longtime friend, Mary Frances Jessee Tiller, and I stay in touch via phone.) No one knows you better than friends you've known since grade school and high school. Yes, we hold many of each other's secrets never to be shared.

Being in high school in the 1950s, we were the generation that introduced rock and roll into our culture. At the Patio Restaurant, another teen gathering place (along with "the pharmacy" and Mutt and Jeff's), we danced over and over to Bill Haley and the Comets' "Rock Around the Clock." It was the first rock-and-roll song I was exposed to, and we teens loved it. If the "macho" boys wouldn't dance with us, then we girls danced with each other. Didn't matter to us.

Another fond memory from high school is the fact that some of my friends and I would meet on Pricie Stewart's front porch to play the card game Rook almost every afternoon after school. We became really expert players of that game. I probably could have used that time to study, but playing Rook with friends was far more fun.

I suppose this is a good place to mention that I was a majorette in the Pennington High School Marching Band. As with my math skills, I wasn't the greatest majorette, but adequate to hold the position. One reason might be that other girls didn't covet marching around in short skirts in parades or on a football field in subzero weather. Our uniforms were much more modest in those days than the skimpy ones worn today. Our formal winter uniform was a long-sleeved wool outfit with fur (fake I'm sure) around the bottom of the skirt and fur hats with a plume and boots with tassels. (See photo section for that now-ancient costume.) Our less formal uniform was a letter sweater (with blouse underneath) and a short corduroy skirt.

One memory from that time is much less fun. After graduating high school I attended Knoxville Business College, and while home for a visit one weekend I got a call from a woman telling me that I had a stalker. The caller was the aunt of the young man who was stalking me, and she said that he had hitchhiked to Knoxville several times trying to find me. According to her, his attraction to me had started when he'd seen me as a majorette and continued. Being young and stupid enough to be unconcerned, I just laughed it off and thought no more about it. But after I'd gone back to school, the aunt realized I hadn't taken her seriously and called my mother, who of course was terrified for me. The aunt must have thought there was reason to fear, or she wouldn't have called to report a relative, but I am thankful that he never found me.

Of course we teens were as delusional as most, and we considered ourselves the most cool and daring people on planet earth. Recalling the antics I got into now, some seem as silly as they were, some even dangerous, but the world has changed and seems far more dangerous now than in the days of Ozzie and Harriet and calico skirts, when fishing and hunting were the most dangerous things to do. As far as I ever knew, drugs were never an issue at that time and place.

My friend Sue Yates (now deceased) and I once decided to sneak into the annual Lee County Fair without paying. Now why on God's green earth we decided to do that I have no idea, because we had the money to pay for a ticket. Regardless, that was our decision that night. So, of course, the good-natured local policeman (more Andy Griffith than Barney Fife) caught and stopped us, which made us more determined. Later, when we ran into him on the concourse, he laughingly said, "I'll bet a dollar to a donut that y'all didn't pay to get in." He was right, of course, and we felt some pride in our silly antics.

On another occasion, Sue and I decided to hitchhike. Again, stupid idea, but we managed to do it without getting ourselves killed or raped. We hitchhiked from Pennington Gap, Virginia, to Big Stone Gap, Virginia, all of nineteen miles away. The couple who picked us up was having a good time, with some alcohol involved, and dropped us off at the local drive-in restaurant. There were always folks from Pennington being served by the carhops, so thankfully we found a ride home with familiar faces.

Definitely the most dangerous adventure that I was involved in was the day several girlfriends, myself, and at least one Boy Scout, David Kesner, went into the massive, unexplored caves and caverns that range below the town. To this day, I don't know just how large the caverns are, but as an adult with some amount of sense, I know that our adventure had the potential to end in disaster. This is another of the times in my life that I believe the good Lord was watching over me.

The opening to the cave was small enough that we had to crawl on our bellies to enter. I'm so claustrophobic today that I can't do a closed MRI, so I can't imagine how I managed that feat. The Boy Scout had a flashlight and had been in there before, so I'm sure he guided us with more authority than he actually possessed. Needless to say, it was dark, and we maneuvered on ledges high enough that we would drop a pebble and have to wait a few seconds before we'd hear it hit bottom. In one cavern there were pools of green water that of course we drank from. All this gives me the creeps just thinking of the danger now, but after spending several hours in that cave we made it out, covered from head to toe in mud. We had to trudge through town on our way home looking like mud monsters, and were met with horror and terror in the hearts of our parents.

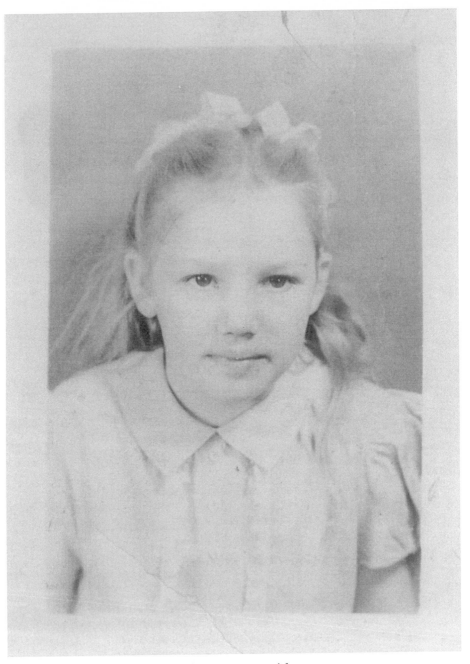

Nina as a young girl

Chapter Four
Dad's Family, the Stacys

My paternal grandparents, Mollie Jane Kirk Stacy and Andrew Jackson Stacy, were a different breed than my maternal grandparents (Ruby Barlow King and Murphy King). The Stacys were Methodists and Republican, while the Kings were Baptists and Democrats. It brought about no conflict for me, because I was too young to vote, and any church debate was solved much later when I married into the Thomas family. They were Methodists, and I found myself more comfortable with that denomination. I've always been registered as a Democrat and remain so, though nothing is ever as "cut and dried" as folks in both parties seem to think, and I've been known to vote a split ticket when rationality dictated. I can assure you that my vote has been Democratic for presidential elections, and certainly for the most recent one.

In my young life, my mother (Virginia Lou), brother (Jack King Stacy), and I lived with my King grandparents, therefore I had a closer relationship with them; but since both families lived in my hometown, I was fortunate to have lots of interaction with both. I called the Stacy grandparents Nana (we pronounced Nannie) and Granddaddy. Nana outlived Granddaddy by twenty years. Nana was a force to reckon with—in a good way.

My parents were divorced when I was very young (five years old), and I had very little interaction with my father. Dad served in the air force and lived on the West Coast. The final state was California, where he raised another family with his wife, Cynthia Crosby Stacy, and their four children: Andrea, Lee, Susan, and Michael.

The first lengthy trip that I remember taking to visit my father was to Albuquerque, New Mexico, where he was stationed at the time. I think I was about ten years old. He had driven to Virginia for a visit and invited my cousin Millard Robbins, a few years older, and myself to drive back to New Mexico with him for a short visit. I don't remember much about the visit, but I remember the plane ride back home. It was my first time flying, and it was in a propeller plane. I was airsick, throwing up all the way home. Poor Millard had no idea what to do with me, especially when I locked myself in the bathroom and the stewardess (as they were called at the time) had to coax me out. When we finally landed at the Bristol VA/TN airport (the closest commercial airport to my little hometown), my mother and Millard's mother met us, and were both of the opinion that I was the most pathetic, disheveled-looking girl they'd ever seen. I couldn't have looked any worse than I felt.

Another of my trips (years later) to visit Dad was with his sister, my Aunt Ida; Millard's sister, my cousin Jane; and Nana. I might add that all the Stacys were "characters" in that they had a very dry sense of humor that hit my funny bone. This trip was before cars had air-conditioning, but it was summer when we headed from Virginia to California. I was about sixteen years old. There is a photo of me sitting on a large piece of petrified wood in the Petrified Forest we visited on that trip. A note aside, this trip was made before my cousin Roger Rector (from the King side of the family) was superintendent of the Petrified Forest National Park, which occurred years later. I believe his whole career was with the National Park Service. No clue where he is now.

Along the way, we encountered a car with a lone man that kept passing us and then slowing down. Aunt Ida would then pass him and so on, until Aunt Ida realized what he was doing. He was trying to expose himself to a carload of women. When Aunt Ida realized what he was doing, she opted not to pass him again and, thinking Nana's curiosity would get the better of her, warned her *not* to look at him. She explained that he was an exhibitionist. Of course, neither Nana nor I had ever heard of an exhibitionist, so Ida enlightened us. After we arrived back in Virginia, Nana was telling a friend about the event. She couldn't quite remember the word exhibitionist, so told her friend that we'd seen a "demonstrator." Nana never let a faulty memory detract from a good story.

Another humorous event remembered from that trip happened when we stopped for a bathroom break at a filling station in Texas. Aunt Ida and Jane went in before Nana and me. When they came out they were giggling, and maiden Aunt Ida was jokingly saying, "Well if I'd had a quarter, I'd have bought me one." More giggling. Again they had to explain to Nana and me that there had been a prophylactics machine in the ladies room. Of course, Nana and I had no idea what that was either. Using more common words, they explained that a machine sold condoms in the ladies room. Those Texas women must have been far more advanced than we Appalachians.

Because we were children of divorce, my brother and I shared Christmas with both sets of grandparents. Since we spent Christmas mornings with the King grandparents, Mother, Jack King, and I always went to Nana Stacy's farm for Christmas Eve parties. (See photo section.) Almost all Stacys were present: aunts, uncles, cousins, and grandparents, as well as those living out of town. The Christmas Eve party was looked on with some excitement and some dread by the females. It was nice to exchange gifts, eat the goodies, and drink Nana's eggnog before the men started adding their libations to it.

Christmas Eve was special to Nana because it was her wedding anniversary. The story goes that on December 24, 1907, she and Granddaddy eloped. She had told her parents that she and her younger sister, Callie, were going to visit friends when she was actually meeting Jack to elope. They left on the train headed for Cumberland Gap, where Mollie and Jack were married. They spent the night at a hotel there. The next day after dinner, Jack went to a grocery store and brought back a bag of white grapes. (I think they must have been green grapes they called white, but not sure.) Millie had never eaten white grapes, and this started a love of them that lasted for the rest of her life. On December 26, 1907, they rode the train back to Pennington Gap and went by horse and buggy to Ely's Creek to tell their families they were married. The marriage lasted until Granddaddy's death in 1972.

For each Christmas Eve party, Uncle Ed was sent to cut the Christmas tree from somewhere on the farm or in the wooded area on the little mountain foothill nearby. Uncle Ed was a farmer, hunter, and fisherman, thus he did not share the same aesthetics the women of the family did. It seemed as though he tried to find the ugliest tree imaginable (think Charlie Brown). I've wondered if he did it deliberately to annoy his sisters, because he never escaped negative comments from them. Nana could have cared less, if she even noticed. She was probably too busy adding a thimble full of liquor to the eggnog, giggling while thinking she was doing something mischievous. Unbeknownst to her, the men had already added their bit of mischief to the eggnog—which was a tad more than a thimble full.

Dad always sent a box of gifts for everyone. Some of his gifts consisted of jewelry or other items that he had made or items that he thought we would like. Some we did, some not so much, but at least he'd made the effort. Nana usually gave the children silver dollars. Some were old (dated in the 1800s), and some I still have.

The one tradition that the women dreaded about the party came from Aunt Ginny's husband, Uncle Melvin. For some ungodly reason, he thought it was cute to pinch women on the behind. If we dared to protest, it seemed to make it more humorous, so we felt obliged to laugh along with him. Aunt Ginny would have taken offense had we not, and it didn't seem worth a family feud for us to protest too much. If there was mistletoe over the door (and there always was), he would catch my attractive mother and dramatically bend her over for a kiss. She hated it, but again Melvin and Aunt Ginny found it humorous. They apparently didn't realize that none of the rest of the women in the family shared their humor— or maybe that's why it was so funny to them. Thankfully, he never went beyond the pinches and the dreaded kiss, because we would not have tolerated anything more invasive than that.

Dad, Jack Kirk Stacy, was one of five siblings along with Ida, Gladys, Ed, and Virginia (Aunt Ginny). Uncle Ed was married to a wonderfully sweet woman, Aunt Marie, and they had three boys:

Edward, Robert, and Frank. Unfortunately Frank died in a car crash at a young age.

Aunt Ida lived a lot of her life in our small town of Pennington Gap, Virginia. She worked as a schoolteacher. She never married, but did treat her many nephews and nieces as her children by re-membering our birthdays each year with a twenty-dollar bill in our birthday cards. She helped in other ways when needed as well. I had her for a teacher in high school history. I can assure you that she made sure not to show favoritism toward me.

Aunt Gladys married Millard Robbins, a dentist (we referred to him as "Uncle Doc"), and they lived in Pennington Gap as well. They had four children: Millard, Jane, Rebecca, and Andrew. It was a nice perk for me to have access to free dental care as a child. Their children were talented, smart, and since Rebecca was crowned Queen of the Lee County Fair in 1963, they could also lay claim to being a good-lookin' lot as well.

Aunt Ginny married Melvin Willey, who worked at Oak Ridge, Tennessee. They lived in nearby Knoxville with their sons, John and Richard. At the time, Melvin was not allowed to talk about what they did at Oak Ridge, because it was a government facility and very little information was forthcoming about the goings-on there. Of course, we now know that it was the place where the atomic bomb was built. We were aware that he was very intelligent and had probably more than one invention registered to his name. As far as I know, his inventions had nothing to do with the atomic bomb. Except for his pinching at Christmas parties, Melvin was a nice, likable man. When he died, he donated his body to what's known as "The Body Farm" in Knoxville. The "Farm" is where they do forensic anthropologic research at the University of Tennessee when people donate their bodies for scientific research. Aunt Ginny was talented in artistic ways. She decorated eggs similar to the well-known Russian eggs and had hundreds of them showcased in cab-inets in her house as well as giving them as gifts to family members.

When Nana opened the first flower shop in town, Ginny also became talented at flower design and arranging. All the Stacy women worked there on and off when needed, meaning when there was a funeral or wedding. Sometimes on weekends, Nana would call me to help as well. I was only allowed to prepare greenery to go into the arrangements. That consisted of clamping leaf stems together with a little machine. It was really boring and I hated it, plus Nana only paid me one dollar per day for all my hours at a boring task. As the saying goes, Nana knew how to "hold on to a dollar." She came from a poor family, so she was frugal. She told a story about being a little girl looking forward to going to her aunt's house and being treated to cornbread with honey on it. The honey was her sweet treat. Years later, she kept beehives on her farm.

Nana was a "women's libber" before the term existed. She did not like housework, so she always had a hired woman to help around the house. One of the structures on the farm was a small house for one of the women, named Eunie, who worked for her. That little house was forever after referred to as the "Eunie house" long after Eunie was gone. (See photos of Nana and farmhouse.)

Nana's farm, Willow Springs Farm, was so called because it had a natural spring on it along with weeping willow trees. There was a springhouse where the water running through it was cold enough to use as a refrigerator. When Nana had a dairy farm that supplied milk to town folks, they used to keep the milk cold in the springhouse until delivery. They supplied milk and butter to Mama King's house. The milk was in glass bottles with two to three inches of cream on top. During that time oleo margarine had come into being, but having eaten Nana's butter, I refused to eat anything but real butter for years. Also in summer, Nana kept watermelons in the springhouse. Those were the juiciest melons from her garden and the coldest from the spring. There was also a creek that ran through the farm where Native Americans used to camp. Over the years, when Uncle Ed and his crew would plow for a garden, they would find many arrowheads in each furrow.

Nana preferred auctions to housework, buying and selling livestock for the farm. She bought houses around town to rent. She bought a second farm that eventually was owned by Aunt Ida. The reason for the second farm, and I'm only assuming here, was to have a second place on which to raise tobacco. The law in Virginia dictated that farmers could only raise a certain amount of tobacco on each farm. During those times, tobacco was a lucrative product sold to the North Carolina cigarette companies. Each fall farmers took their tobacco to warehouses to sell.

Nana's farm was backed up to a foothill belonging to the Cumberland Mountain range. The top was level enough to have a small airport on top. I don't know if she rented the land for that use or just how that operation worked, but it was only used for small, personal planes that very few folks in those parts could afford. It is no longer in use as far as I know, but it was fairly busy for a few years back then.

Nana, Ida, Gladys, and Ginny all loved antiques. Their houses were filled with them, and when Nana's buying started overflowing onto the back porch, my ever-industrious Nana opened an antique shop.

The grown women in the family had lots of funny sayings. They apparently had a friend named Ethel who sometimes repeated things she shouldn't. So when one of the sisters was about to share something the others thought she shouldn't, they'd quietly whisper to her, "Hush your mouth, Ethel." The family tale goes that my young cousin, John (Ginny's son), picked up on this before he could speak plainly. He once said something like "Bel-mel-ful," which they finally figured out was his attempt at "Hush your mouth, Ethel." This gave them a good word to use instead of the whole phrase. They started saying "Bel-mel-ful" to shut up a too-gabby sister, and a non-family member was none the wiser that they were telling the sister to shut up.

When I was still in high school, Nana regularly tried to fix me up with a rich boyfriend. Her motto was, "It's as easy to love a rich man as a poor one." (I wish I'd listened to her!) One she had in mind was a young man from a rather well-to-do family living in the area. I hesitate to use the word wealthy, because I don't really know how wealthy or not they were. Regardless, this young man had dated my mother's sister (Aunt Peggy at one time), so I know the age difference would not have been an appropriate match for a high school girl, but that didn't deter Nana. She'd see me in town and embarrass me by yelling, "I saw Billy Joe [not his real name] today!" I'd think, *Oh dear Lord, please let her not have said anything in reference to a relationship with me.* My only hope was that he never knew of her hoped-for matchup.

One of the family secrets that Cousin Millard shared with me (much later in life and just before his death) was the fact that Nana's mother had been in the mental institution in Marion, Virginia, for a period of time. I don't have too much information about this, because most people I could ask about it are now dead, but I do know that at least a couple of my cousins have suffered with debilitating depression. I too have suffered depression on various occasions, though not debilitating. It is only supposition on my part, but I suspect that Nana's mother probably suffered depression before much was known of how to treat it. Regardless of what I know or don't know about her mother, Nana lived a full and interesting life. Nana lived to see her one hundred fourth birthday. When she reached her hundredth, the family had a celebration for her, and most folks in town were invited, and most came. It was reported with photos in our hometown newspaper, the *Powell Valley News*. That year she was grand marshal in the annual Tobacco Festival Parade, which was also reported in the PVN. She loved all the attention and expected a grand party each year afterward. (See photos and newspaper description.)

I've shared some of my father's history of womanizing before, and I think Nana and especially Aunt Ida tried to make up for some of his abandonment of my brother, Jack King, and me. I still have trouble with some of the things my dad did. For example, when Nana was in her nineties, he decided it was time to introduce her (and the rest of the Virginia family) to the son he had living in Texas, named Jack Kirk Stacy Jr. This son, Jack Jr., was conceived years before in another relationship Dad had while married to my mother (an infamous debacle in Louisiana described later). I had tolerated many of the hurtful things my dad had done over the years, but a secret son topped the scale even for Dad. So I wrote him a letter telling him how self-centered he was and how inconsiderate of the feelings of others, including the son we'd never met, to have kept that a secret all these years. It was a long letter, and I don't remember all the things I said about years of resentment, but I never heard from my father again.

That son, Jack Jr., did eventually make an effort to meet the family and has been to visit me on occasion when he travels. I find him to be a very nice man and have enjoyed learning more about him and his family.

Dad's will reflected his neglect of my brother and me, and I'm assuming Jack Jr. also. Since he had contributed nothing (to my knowledge) to my brother, Jack King, and me while we were growing up, I did not expect anything from him in death, and that's basically what we got. The small amount he left us did not make up for a lifetime of neglect. No use to fret about something that was no surprise, better just to let it go.

But, back to Nana, I will never forget the eulogy the preacher read at her funeral.

I am quoting from the minister's words when he stood at the podium, and his first words were, "This is a celebration." Then he continued to say that rather than mourn her death, we should celebrate her having lived 104 years.

At the grave site the minister continued:

> Mollie Kirk Stacy was born in 1887. Grover Cleveland was president. She was alive when twenty presidents moved into the White House. She was nine years old when Henry Ford built and ran the first car. She was eleven when Teddy Roosevelt led the charge up San Juan Hill. She was twelve when aspirin was invented. She was nineteen when two brothers named Wright in North Carolina flew an airplane for three minutes. She was thirty-one when Armistice Day proclaimed the end

of WWI. She was forty-two for the stock market crash in 1929. She was eighty-two when the astronauts walked on the moon.

He concluded by saying:

In a day when yesterday seems like ancient history and tomorrow looks like a futuristic painting, it somehow brings a measure of assurance to witness across a century and four years a life testifying that God is the same yesterday, today, and forever.

*Sixteen-year-old Nina on a trip with Aunt Ida, cousin Jane,
and Nana at Petrified Forest*

*Nana and Granddaddy Stacy
on their wedding day*

Young Mollie

Christmas Eve party at Nana's farm c. 1950.
Brother Jack on bike, cousin Rebecca's back to camera,
Nina on floor in foreground, cousin Jane Robbins behind Nina,
Nana Stacy behind Jane, Aunts Ida, Gladys, and Nina's mother
"Jenny Lou" standing in back, Aunt Ginny Willey seated in chair
to the right. Many other relatives in attendance not pictured.
Probably gathered around the punch bowl and food in the dining
room and kitchen.

Granddaddy Stacy. I'm
sure the dog's name
was Spot. If he'd been
brown, Nana would
have named him
"Brownie."

Nana Stacy (Mollie Kirk Stacy) celebrating her 100th birthday

Nana and Granddaddy Stacy's farmhouse on Willow Springs Farm

100th Birthday

Mollie Stacy celebrated her 100th birthday Saturday, November 7, with a reception at the home of Gladys Robbins in Pennington Gap, where she received more than 120 guests, including local family members as well as those from as far away as Baltimore and Atlanta. She received cards from President and Nancy Reagan, Senator John Warner, TV personality Willard Scott, and many more from friends and relatives, along with lots of flowers. She said her mother told her she was born about 4:00 a.m. on election day, the first time her father, M.R. Kirk, voted. He walked seven miles to vote she said. She was the first woman to register to vote at St. Charles after the 19th Amendment, allowing women to vote, became law August 26, 1920. She said she has never missed voting and thinks everybody should do so. She was told she is the oldest registered woman voter in Lee County. Looking pretty and smiling, with a bouquet of roses on her hand Saturday, she said, shyly, "I've got a lot to smile about for someone 90 years old."

Clipping from town newspaper, Mollie at 100th birthday party

Cousins on vacation, starting front to left: Mollie Rorrer Gore, Robyn Rorrer Puryer, Rachel Robbins, Karen Robbins Cole, Nina, and Rebecca Robbins

L–R: Karen Cole, Robyn Puryer, Nina, Rebecca Robbins,
Mollie Gore

Aunt Virginia (Ginny) Stacy and Uncle Melvin Willey's wedding c. 1945 on Nana's farm. L–R: Ann Newman, Aunt Ginny, Melvin, and Uncle "Doc" Millard Robbins. Front: cousin Jane Robbins, Nina, cousin Millard Robbins.

Chapter Five
Marriage, Divorce, and Cancer

When you hear the word marriage, you tend to think of love and hopefully "happily ever after." In reality, it is two people who are forming a union that brings together each's past baggage and any insecurities in hopes of blending into a workable relationship. When the word divorce is mentioned, you can bet some drama is to follow.

What a dilemma! Some things are difficult to explain—like an unsuccessful marriage, ultimate divorce, and cancer. Those were three of life's obstacles that I faced around the same time and overcame. The fact is that I have not given much thought to any of them in many years, but in thinking back . . . it's complicated. On the bright side, divorce turned out to be a good thing for me. Granted, I fought it at first, but ultimately it was the psychological boost that propelled me forward to achieve a better, more fulfilling life.

My original reason for writing a memoir was to reveal parts of my life that my son, Eric, and grandson, Ethan, might not know and might eventually find interesting. Or maybe not. Who knows? And as for Eric and Ethan's reading some facts about my past and not entirely perfect relationship with Bill, it should not reflect on their very good relationship with him. They love him, and I once loved him enough to marry him, but that leaves some drama when divorce happens. He was and is a good father and grandfather. In fact, the saying "tragedy plus time equals comedy" comes to mind when I think of my marriage to Bill. So I'll start with that in mind and try to keep it as painless as possible. Also, it is worth mention here that we often find ourselves in family gatherings with our son and grandson and on Grandparents Day. In these situations, it's all cool, calm, and copacetic.

Saying that reminds me of my favorite old joke: "It just dawned on me why Mayberry was so peaceful and quiet—nobody was married. Here are the single people that come to mind: Andy, Aunt Bea, Barney, Floyd, Howard, Goober, Gomer, etc. In fact, the only one married was Otis, and he stayed drunk all the time."

In an attempt to be fair and get feedback, I invited Bill to read this manuscript before I published it. I think he dreaded it, but he finally agreed to read it, and both my friend Debby Miller (who arrived at my house right after he'd read it) and I were pleased at his first reaction, which was: "It is more fair than I deserve." And he added that folks grow up and change as they get older, or words to that effect. However, after a week or so of thinking about it, he asked me to remove a couple of things I'd written about him, and I have done that. I hated to do it, because that was what I thought was some "fun stuff" about him, but in exchange, I asked if he wanted to write the foreword. I thought it only fair that he be given a forum in which to respond. I agree with most of what he said, especially about the fragility of memory, and I'll admit that his is much better than mine; however, because of that I've always kept written records in the form of journals and letters for reference. So keep that in mind, and I'm sure it will all even out.

Bill had a successful career as a political science professor at Georgia State University, where he was apparently a great teacher, but as with everyone, including myself, he does have some warts. Bill always made sure to be as charming as needed to impress along with his good deeds.

So what was my initial interest in Bill as a young man? His face had a nice square jawline that even the actor Kevin Costner, owner of a weak jawline, would envy. I suppose it boils down to youthful superficiality, because it was Bill's nice looks that attracted me initially. Also, it was obvious that he was intelligent and most likely had a good future ahead of him. That was appealing, though during the time he was drinking, which was much of our marriage, it's safe to say some of the appeal wore off. That is not to imply that I didn't do my share of drinking, but my drinking did not manifest itself in the same way as his. I was mainly hurt when he flirted with other women at parties, and obviously my insecurity came into play. In reading this, I wonder why I didn't see the danger signs of an unhealthy relationship long before it came to marriage, but youthful ignorance is all I can come up with.

As for *my* troubles and woes, I often had a weight problem, which caused unhappiness for both Bill and me. Stress eating would bring on weight, so it was a never-ending battle for me. Sometimes I'd win and sometimes not. To try to alleviate the problem, I once went to a doctor to get diet pills, which were effective. I think they must have been what are called "uppers," because they made me work like a possessed woman and forget to eat. The problem was that they caused side effects. After taking them for a while, I started having anxiety attacks, so the doctor took me off the pills.

Before going on, I must say that if I'd been asked during the time the divorce was in progress or soon after, I'd have blamed Bill for all the problems. I'll also admit that I did not handle the situation well. I make no apology to anyone except my son, Eric, for having to endure my craziness at the time and for being of little comfort to him. I'm ashamed of that, but I was going through all the feelings of grief that come into play in one's psyche when feeling unlovable, disposable, and rejected: disbelief, hurt, fear, heartbreak, an uncertain future, and anger, just to name a few. Though Bill was responsible for many of the problems, certainly infidelity, I realize that my past came into play as well. I came into the relationship and marriage as an insecure young woman, especially where men were concerned. My expectations of a healthy relationship were probably predetermined. I may have been attracted to Bill because he was reminiscent of the description of my womanizing father. Did I think I could marry someone like my father and fix or overcome what little I knew about Mother's experience? What was in my mind is still uncertain to me even now, but give me a break—it happened long ago, and I'd forgotten most of it until I started writing a memoir.

I grew up with a wonderful, caring, loving mother, but one who had had such a traumatic experience with her first marriage that it left her understandably scarred and bitter. She would never have knowingly done anything that would scar me. She spent her life devoted to my brother, Jack, and me, but I must have absorbed some of her hurt into my subconscious. She was not one who openly discussed her fears or problems; she tended to keep such things to herself. Never did I hear her talk ill about anyone, and even if I asked, she refused to discuss anything about my father. The only advice about men from my mother was, *"Men—you can't trust them,"* throughout my teen years. I know in her kind heart that she meant this to make me cautious and keep me free of hurt.

Obviously I was curious about what had happened to cause divorce between my parents. Family members had shared bits and pieces but never the whole story. I don't know if they knew the whole story or thought it better for me not to know. All I knew was that there had been an incident in Louisiana where possibly three women had been involved. Mother and Dad's sister, Aunt Gladys, had gone to keep my unfaithful, womanizing father out of the brig. I've since learned what happened and have a better understanding of Mother's heartbreak, which I will share a bit later. It is so convoluted that it deserves its own chapter.

My early relationships in high school were interesting to revisit. I had no idea how to interact with the male gender. I knew from Mother's admonitions what I should and should not do, and that was my mode of operation. It was the '50s, after all, and I was trained to be "a nice girl." Besides, we attended the First Baptist Church and I heard hellfire and damnation every Sunday. Now, I'm here to tell you that that will get a young girl's attention! I'm aware of how boring this sounds in today's world, but I was a product of my upbringing and environment of the time, and thus offer no apologies.

The guys I dated had to be satisfied that necking or making out (as we called it then) was as far as they were going to get with me. I think even in high school I was attracted to guys who had a reputation as "ladies' men" types, as my father had been described. I suppose Sigmund Freud comes into play here, because I was attracted to boys like my womanizing father. The endings of those relationships were uneventful, but they tended to support Mother's admonitions about men not being trustworthy.

Once, I bragged to girlfriends, with much more bravado than I actually felt (which was often the case), that I would pursue and win a relationship with a particular guy. I did start dating the young man, who was not a womanizing sort and seemed totally interested in just me. That must have scared me to death, because I made sure to sabotage the relationship and break up with him. Looking back, I regret that, because he did not deserve that treatment and I remember him fondly.

Now, back to my relationship with Bill. In hindsight, I realize that the marriage was probably doomed from the beginning. We were not a good match, but it took years to finally discover that we weren't. It seemed perfect at first. I was a small-town girl from Appalachia whose formative years happened in the 1950s. He was raised in Appalachia, the oldest of eight children (Bill, Joe, Gerald, Bobby, Johnny, Jimmy, Mary, and Evelyn), on a farm with a terrific family much like mine. I adored his family and still do, though time and distance interfere. His mother and I were especially close. Naomi Van Lear Thomas was a special lady known as "Van" or "Mom T" to us daughters-in-law. She once told me (during the pending divorce), "You and I aren't divorcing each other." She and I communicated with letters and birthday cards until her death. I have fond memories of sitting in her farmhouse kitchen in great conversation, watching and learning while she cooked. She was one of those cooks who could take nothing and make something delicious out of it. Being the mother of eight children, she had to be creative as well as frugal. Of course she had a garden and canned food for winter. An example of her creativity is that if, say, she cooked a turkey, she could fix meals with leftovers for a week. First would be the meal where the turkey was served along with side dishes. Then might come a meal with turkey salad or turkey hash. After that she'd cook the turkey bones in water for a broth that would turn into a delicious soup when vegetables and herbs were added.

Bill's home was only about one hundred miles from mine,

though we didn't know each other until we'd both left home in search of our futures.

We met in Knoxville, Tennessee. He was in his senior year at the University of Tennessee, and I was just out of Knoxville Business College and working in a business office. Truthfully, it is all pretty vague in my memory now, but I think we had some mutual friends when we met and started dating. The dates mostly involved partying with friends, with lots of beer drinking involved. After reading this, Bill reminded me that we often went to the American Legion on Alcoa Highway in Knoxville. Again, his memory is much better than mine.

I've no idea the amount of time between dating and getting more serious, but there came a time when I wanted commitment or I was going to move on, so he proposed. It wasn't romantic or with a ring, just a proposal in his car, as I remember it. But I was a happy girl, because it seemed like it was time to make such commitments.

Being a girl of the '50s meant that I had certain expectations of what one should do, and that would be to start with marriage and a family. You know, June Cleaver and all the sitcoms of perfect marriages and family of that era. Later, after the children were of age, I would complete my dream of going to college for the art degree that I had yet to attain.

Business college was Mother's idea, because, I'm sure, that's what she could afford. God bless her. She did the best she could for me, and I continue to be grateful for her, but business school was not my forte. I still dreamed of art school at some point.

The fact that Bill and I didn't have much in common did not occur to me. He had his sights on continuing his education toward a career in political science, which held little interest for me. He was a smart guy, so why not? He also had an interest in sports and a memory about sports like an encyclopedia. Sports did not hold my interest either, though we did attend many UT football games. The crowd and beer usually entertained me more than the game. He seemed to have more of a vision for his future than I did. I was willing to follow in the background, being the supportive wife and thinking we were working on our future, not just his.

We lived in several different states while he chased his career dreams. Right after he graduated from UT, Bill wanted a new experience and sought a job in California. As newlyweds, we decided to do just that. (See early-marriage trip to California.) After about a year in California, we produced an adorable human being: our son, Eric. This was probably the happiest time of our marriage and when I was the most content.

Having Eric was a joy, and though Bill seemed happy about the baby, he showed a lack of sensitivity to me at times. Eric was born on December 30, which means the next night was New Year's Eve. I expected that since I'd just given birth to our son, Bill would want to celebrate New Year's Eve with me in the hospital, but he opted to go to his office party instead. I was still young and optimistic, so I hid the hurt of a lonely New Year's Eve. I don't see Bill as a bad person. Insensitive or lacking common sense at times, perhaps, but not bad. I've found that sensitivity seems to be a missing gene for a lot of guys, so maybe it was just a guy thing.

Without going into each and every place we lived, with many more tales to match, here is a brief synopsis. After California, we were back in Knoxville for Bill to complete his master's degree at UT. Upon completing that degree, he wanted to follow his favorite professor, Richard Cortner, to the University of Arizona in Tucson for his doctorate. I was willing to follow him in pursuit of these degrees, still thinking we were working on our future together.

In Tucson I was again a bit out of my element, 2,500 miles away from friends and family. I was isolated from everything familiar to me. I must admit that I was a tad uncomfortable at first being among his friends, who were intellectuals far above my education level. They did nothing to make me feel inferior, and in fact I remained long-distance friends with many of them even after we'd moved away and divorced. However, at the time, I'd hear words thrown around like "existentialism" and would have no idea what they were talking about. I'm not sure they did either, because it seemed that they were trying to figure out exactly what the word meant as well. My plan was to eventually catch up by completing my college degree at some point after Bill had a job and we were settled.

Tucson was our final destination before Bill completed his doctorate and we moved to Atlanta. However, Tucson did offer an education of sorts for me as well. It was the 1960s, and it was becoming fairly obvious that Bill and I were not necessarily in the same "groove," to borrow a word from that era. Remember, I was a girl brought up in a small town in the June Cleaver '50s and was shocked at some of the events happening—free love, drugs, hippies. I wasn't all that old, but I still held some of the naïveté and values of my upbringing, though Lord knows I tried to keep up by at least dressing the part—the bell bottoms, sandals, and such that Bill and his classmates were wearing. That's not to say that I totally understood a lot of what was going on, but like Bob Dylan's song of the time: "The Times They Are A-Changin'."

On one occasion, I was part of a mixture of female students and friends while the men were off for another event. The group I was with decided to drop acid. No way was I going to do that, and I was the only one in the room who didn't participate. To their credit, I was not judged or reprimanded by the group for not partaking. But there I sat with a room full of women on an LSD acid trip that I was not enjoying. I have no way of knowing if they enjoyed a trip as described in Tom Wolfe's *The Electric Kool-Aid Acid Test* that immortalized Ken Kesey. There were no vivid colors floating in front of my eyes, and I was not on an imaginary "flying" trip anywhere. If any of them had a psychedelic epiphany afterward, I'm not aware of it. I was just sitting there unaware of their trip experiences (bored stiff, frankly) while waiting for the women to come back down to earth and the men to return so I could go home and go to bed. And dad-gum-it, the chairs weren't even comfortable! I can promise you that it was not one of my more enjoyable evenings.

Bill and I did try weed a few times, and all that did for me was make me sleepy and hungry. Since I had to fight a weight problem, I soon decided that weed was not my friend. That is the only drug I was ever willing to try, unless you consider alcohol a drug.

While in Tucson, I did have reason to wonder what was going on many times. Bill was working on his doctorate, so it stands to reason that he needed to study. He went to school every day. I think he might have come home for dinner and then left again every night saying he was going to study with friends . . . or just to study. I can't remember all the reasons given now. Regardless, he didn't return home until late at night, and with evidence of drinking on his breath. Any hanky-panky going on? I've no clue, but with my insecurity still in play, it did make me wonder.

Bill took a job at Georgia State University in Atlanta after completing his doctorate. Few students in the '60s wanted to move south, but being Southerners, we were glad for the employment there.

It was in Atlanta that Bill eventually had one affair that I can document. It was with a married graduate student, whom I'll call Judy, who had a baby still in diapers. I don't know if she was one of his students or just a student in that department.

Of course the affair got my attention, and I was off on another diet to lose weight—which I did. That seemed to do the trick eventually, though Judy warned him that I'd surely gain the weight back. I doubt that weight was the only reason for the affair to begin with, but losing it seemed to help. I was very thin (size 8-ish). The truth of the matter was that it was healthier for me to lose the weight, but not the reason for it. When was I going to wake up to a hopeless marriage and get back my dignity and self-worth? It was going to take a while longer, but it did happen.

An Appalachian meme comes to mind that says: *"Mamaw always said, 'What feels like rejection is often God's protection when you're heading in the wrong direction.'"* Why couldn't I have heard and absorbed that before the marriage? I wouldn't have listened, of course. In fact, I recently came across a carefully worded letter from Mama King written before the marriage listing some things I should consider before getting married and hinting that I should wait. My precious Mama King just wanted me to know she was thinking of my happiness and welfare. There had been others before the marriage that were dubious about it, but of course I didn't listen to any of them.

After the divorce, Bill ended up marrying yet another graduate student in the department where he taught. That marriage has lasted. Oh, I failed to mention that Bill had stopped drinking either just before our divorce or just after. He actually did change his whole life around by not only stopping drinking, but starting running, and he became a vegetarian. He ran his first Peachtree Road Race during this time. Again, my memory fails when it comes to specific times and years, but he thinks his "clean living" started long before I remember within the marriage. But in case you wonder, I choose to believe that I was not the cause of his drinking, because he was drinking long before I met him. (Note: Bill says, and I quote, "This is definitely true. I think it was probably genetic.")

Regardless, do I have any regrets about my marriage to Bill? No, for several reasons. If you believe that God has a plan for your life, then it was meant to be. If God doesn't have a plan, then it was a learning experience for me. It wasn't all bad (again, see some of our very interesting trips together), and it created the miracles of my son and eventually my grandson. Those two alone would make anything worth it. My description of the marriage is my memory of it and the challenges for me to either cherish or face and overcome. No doubt Bill's memories are probably different, and I've added some notations of his thoughts after he read sections that included him.

I'm foggy on details because it happened so many years ago, but about the same time as the divorce or just after, I came face to face with a cancer diagnosis. Cancer was just another obstacle to overcome, but it was one of the scariest. Just the word cancer struck terror in my heart. Divorce and cancer are both stress inducing. I was devastated emotionally, facing life without the marriage I'd nurtured for sixteen years, and now uncertain how I was going to make a living for my son and myself—assuming I survived cancer. Rejection and disease . . . yeah, I was a tad stressed, but it was not in my nature to let either hurdle defeat me.

When I got the diagnosis of cancer, I was terrified. It was my worst nightmare. While in high school, I'd witnessed the devastation it could wreak on someone. I was taken to visit an uncle who was riddled with cancer and whose body was skeletal. He was unresponsive, lying in bed, obviously near death. That is something that can't be unseen or forgotten, and it never left my psyche. Why I was taken to visit him in that condition is yet another mystery in my past.

I'd been seeing my general doctor and the pap smears were coming up "not negative," but on some sort of scale that meant something to doctors but not to me. To me, the tests were either negative or meant some stage of cancer. Something needed to be done. My nerves were already on edge, and if stress has anything to do with disease, then I was surely the ideal candidate.

I sought a second opinion, but the diagnosis stuck. I had cancer and needed to schedule surgery. The hysterectomy was done at Crawford Long Hospital in Atlanta. Fortunately, the outcome was good, and thank God, I've been cancer free since.

I've written about my early life and feeling abandoned by my father, and now I was facing rejection from my husband. It is no wonder that I might have had some psychological issues, but I just faced them and moved on. It helped that I never lacked love, care, and financial help when needed from my blessed mother, Mama, and Granddaddy King, even while feeling a hole where a father figure should have been. It never kept me from forging on with my life. The emotional consequences of it all left me in a fragile state, but when you have no choice, you trudge on. It's what you do when there's no other choice. As Churchill once said, "Never, never, never give up, except to convictions of honor and good sense." Since Churchill and I share a birthday, I feel a connection with him . . . and his advice.

A favorite of Bill and Eric. Eric was about three or four, I think.

Bill with baby Eric

*Nina with baby Eric
dressed to go somewhere*

*Nina soon after giving birth
to baby Eric in California*

Wedding day, June 1964.
Nina Kirk Stacy and
William R. Thomas Jr.

Nina on her wedding
day (wearing hat
Aunt Gladys insisted
she wear)

Chapter Six
About My Father

Lordy, I hardly know how to describe the man whose sperm helped make me happen. He certainly could never have laid claim to being any sort of father to me, but as you'll see, sperm plays a major role in his life. I will try to explain a rather complicated set of events. Also, I will advise that if this were a movie or a sitcom, one might think it an amusing story, but too exaggerated to be true.

My mother divorced my father, Jack Kirk Stacy, when I was five years old. Mother, Virginia King Stacy, and I lived in Virginia with my maternal grandparents while my so-called father was in the air force stationed in Louisiana. Mother and Dad's sister, my Aunt Gladys, were asked to travel to the base where he was stationed in an effort to keep him out of the brig. Why, you ask? Well, he was involved with two, possibly three, different women, obviously none of whom were his wife, and the air force frowned on such activities. When my sweet, gentle-natured, pregnant mother and her sister-in-law arrived at the base, and according to Mother's companion, my Aunt Gladys, they were met by (or soon learned that there was) another woman who was also pregnant with my father's child. That child would be born two weeks after my brother, Jack *King* Stacy. The other baby was named Jack *Kirk* Stacy Jr. I'm just hoping there are no other Jack Stacys, sired by my father, to be found in the world, but who knows?

Once, when my father was in Virginia visiting his parents, family lore has it the air force called to tell him that his wife in Hawaii had been killed in a car wreck. Which can only mean that I don't dare go to Hawaii and date anyone for fear it might be my half-brother! Whether the tale is true or not, I've no idea, and Ancestry.com wasn't successful in confirming or denying whether this wife ever existed.

Throughout my childhood, this tale and other information regarding my father were not openly shared with me. It was deliberately withheld, probably, because it was thought to be for my own good. I only found out many details after both my parents had passed away. The secrecy made me curious. I contacted the Ancestry.com folks, who have no literal connection with the Mormon Church but sometimes use their data. They are an excellent source for genealogy research and DNA testing. I paid a hefty sum for them to research my father. Other sources used wish not to be named, so I will honor that request.

I've since learned that Cynthia Crosby, whom I always thought was Dad's second wife, was actually one of the women who met Mother and Aunt Gladys when they arrived in Louisiana. I've also learned that there had been several wives in between my mother and Cynthia. Therein lies the aforementioned "set of events."

Mother, Virginia King, was my father's first wife. Then came the incident in Louisiana when Mother and the other pregnant lady, Maureen (last name withheld), met. Mother agreed to a divorce only after my brother was born so that Dad and Maureen could marry in order to legitimize her son. Sometime later, Dad did marry Maureen, and forty-five minutes after the ceremony (I'm told), she left for her hometown. A short time later, she contacted Dad to inform him that she too was applying for divorce.

I'm not sure how much time elapsed before Dad was again involved with multiple women. These were Bernadine and Martha (last names withheld). In court papers found later (by a reliable source), there was an investigation wherein both women claimed to be pregnant by my father. It turned out that Martha was not pregnant. So Dad, thinking Bernadine was pregnant and that he was free, married her. Apparently it did not occur to Dad to check with Maureen for divorce papers before marrying Bernadine. When he did check, he found that there had been no divorce, the reason being that Maureen wanted to divorce him for desertion, which was a two-year process: one year of separation and another year before the divorce could be finalized. He went back to

Bernadine, without explaining the whole story to her (maybe to save embarrassment to her?), and she agreed to give him a divorce. There is no evidence that she was ever pregnant. Eventually he married Cynthia Crosby and lived with her and the four children (Andrea, Lee, Michael, and Susan) they produced for most of the rest of his life. Cynthia eventually divorced him and moved to Oregon with their daughter Andrea.

Dad was a war hero of sorts. I say "of sorts" because he got in and out of trouble with the armed services when he was younger. However, later in his career, he was awarded a Distinguished Flying Cross, Air Medal, and other honorable decorations and had a full military funeral upon his death.

Dad was a bombardier and navigator. He survived five plane crashes during WWII. He was in a coma for six months as a result of the last one, which he wasn't expected to survive. Sources report that he lost much in the service to his country, physically and emotionally. I don't doubt that. I'm told that he rarely spoke of his war experiences but suffered nightmares about them. It was not long before he died (I'm told) that he was finally able to watch the movie *Twelve O'Clock High*. I have no way of knowing if segments of the movie were actually about him and his crew or if the story was just close enough to his experience to be difficult for him to watch. There are records of the fact that he participated in bombing raids over Germany, which would have started from Britain. Whatever the case, he and other soldiers paid a huge price. His tombstone reads: "Peace at Last."

I can feel for the war hero that he became, but I still find it hard to have sympathy for the younger man who left my mother hurt and emotionally damaged. His younger self took "sowing his wild oats" several steps too far, in my estimation. On a lighter note, it would amuse me to think that if karma had been in effect, certain of his very private body parts should have been disabled during the war, but I'm pretty sure those parts were left unharmed.

Whew! If this leaves you confused, just be thankful you weren't left with this hot, crazy mess of a tale to tell about your father.

Since I never actually lived with my father, and had very little relationship with him except at a distance, the legacy he left is a confusing mix of bad and good. My mother, who was a shy, gentle soul, didn't deserve his treatment—nor, for that matter, did any of the other women in his life. She was left with two young children and (as far as I know) with no financial help from him. Lack of a father figure left me with an emotional hole, but I'm also quite certain that I would not have benefited psychologically by living with him. When his whole story was finally revealed to me, it left me with more sympathy for what my mother suffered and a bit more knowledge of the man. Another hurdle, another leap.

Jack Kirk Stacy

Chapter Seven
An Insignificant Affair

After the trauma of divorce and a cancer scare, I was content just to get on with my life without dealing with the male gender for several years. Some of my female friends couldn't live without a man in their life, but I was not one of them. I'd had enough of that grief. The only guy in my life for quite a while was my son, which suited me since he was the love of my life.

Oh, I went out on occasion, but I allowed no serious male connection to happen. Mostly, I hung out with girlfriends, and on one such outing when I was facing my big fiftieth birthday, I went to a bar in Underground Atlanta with my friend Joan to celebrate. Joan was a friend who was never without a guy in her life, so she was usually "on the hunt" when a relationship ended.

This particular night we met a man whom I'll call Nathan and who seemed to be hitting on me. He was entertaining, so both Joan and I enjoyed an evening with him. As Joan and I were leaving, he planted a brief kiss on my lips. It didn't seem aggressive, but was sort of nice and sweet, so I didn't mind. Well, lo and behold, Nathan called me at work the next morning, asked me out, and we started dating. I wasn't too concerned about him, because first, he wasn't my type; second, he was fifteen years younger than me and there was no danger of a long-term relationship. I'd been there and done that, and wanted no part of that kind of heartache again.

This did turn out to be an affair that lasted a bit longer than a year and was just what I needed at the time—good entertainment and good for my self-esteem.

The fact that a younger man was interested in me was flattering to my ego, and the affair with someone much younger taught me some nice, new things in regard to affection. I'll leave it at that.

A bit of information about him that was of no interest to me was that he was into weight training to build a Sylvester Stallone body. Someone had told him he looked like Stallone, which may or may not have been true, but he considered it a compliment. I didn't, because as I said earlier, I'd never been attracted to that type. My dream style was more tall, dark, and handsome Tom Selleck, if I had been on the hunt, which I wasn't. Not to mention the fact that Selleck would have been out of my orb anyway. But that isn't to say I didn't enjoy watching a Rocky movie.

Nathan was in Atlanta attending chiropractic school and would eventually leave for his home in the northeast. He had connections to a chiropractic practice that he would eventually join.

I met a few of his friends while he was in Atlanta, and was not impressed. While we visited one couple, the woman and I were in another room and I went to find Nathan. When I opened the door, he and the guy were snorting cocaine, which was a surprise to me, and just another reason there was not going to be a long-term relationship.

I'd come a long way from my small-town upbringing in the '50s, but doing drugs was not something I would tolerate. Apparently, he knew not to indulge that vice around me, thus his hiding in another room to partake. After he graduated and left to go back home, he would send me plane tickets to come visit, which I did for a while. It was a nice weekend getaway from a stressful work environment. While he was at work during the day, I would entertain myself in downtown Manhattan by visiting art galleries and exploring the city, shopping, and getting plenty of walking exercise. After work he would pick me up and take me to nice restaurants or plays for a fun-filled weekend before I headed back to Atlanta and to work on Monday.

A long-distance relationship with a much younger man who had some disagreeable habits was an interesting experience but also an easy hurdle to jump over, to say "Thanks but no thanks" to and go on with my life.

Chapter Eight
Work Experiences

Other than brief employment experiences before I was married, my work experience started in earnest after my divorce. I've mentioned how devastated I was when faced with divorce. I had yet to get the college degree that I'd envisioned, so the only noticeable skill I had was the fact that I could type. I had, after all, typed the first draft of what would later be my ex-husband's dissertation. The only thing I was left with from that endeavor was an ungrateful ex-husband and an ill temper at the thought of it. That was in the 1960s, before computers were used in every household, and was done on a manual typewriter with carbon paper. If you've never had that experience, thank the good Lord that you were born after that was necessary. It's one of those things of the past that I cringe at the thought of even now.

Not knowing what to do or how I was going to make a living, I volunteered at the church I was attending, the First United Methodist Church in Decatur, Georgia. We'd bought a small bungalow in Decatur, and I received the house in the divorce agreement, which left house payments but no income. I volunteered in the program office, where I was ultimately hired to work with (the late) Kay Burns and the youngest minister on the team, Wiley Stephens. Kay was responsible for organizing volunteers and editing the weekly newsletter, the *Now*.

Among many things this church offered besides ministry was assistance to folks in temporary need of food for themselves or their family. It was a good feeling to be able to help folks in this way. The food pantry was stocked with nonperishable items donated by parishioners.

Kay and Wiley were a joy and made this one of my best work experiences. The senior pastor, Garnett Wilder, wrote a couple of books while I was there and allowed me to design the front covers, which was good use of my God-given artistic ability. The book titles were *Between the Times* and *Promises to Keep*. The people there offered love, emotional support, and a small salary, all of which I needed at the time.

As wonderful as the church job was, it paid very little and I was in need of a better living for Eric and myself. I was struggling financially and living paycheck to paycheck, which didn't always stretch far enough. Bill agreed to pay a small amount of monthly alimony, but it was not nearly enough to pay my bills. He did coach soccer teams to offset the bills for Paideia School, the private school where Eric was enrolled.

My friend Joan Perkins, now deceased, helped me get a job at Georgia State University in the facilities unit of the Division of Continuing Education. Paris Clark was the supervisor who hired me and made it a good experience for us all. He allowed his employees to do their jobs without micromanaging. Mine was to organize room usage, and because I have good organizational skills I was good at the job, which ultimately led to other moves up the GSU ladder.

After being there for a while, I watched with envy as the conference coordinators did their jobs. My job held me to the office manning phones and making reservations most of the time, while the coordinators were free to roam around while doing their seemingly more interesting jobs. Eventually, I applied for and got a job as a conference coordinator. In the real world (outside the university), the job would be called either an event planner or meeting planner and would pay far more money. But I liked and felt secure within the university system.

Again due to my organizational skills, I was good at the job, and my supervisor, Mary Thrift, was again wise enough to give us the freedom to do our jobs without much management. She was terrific at her job and I'm pleased to mention her. When it comes to some of my other supervisors who were not as pleasant, I will not name them for obvious reasons and will use a composite method of description for them. I will also change names plus the composite method to avoid anyone being recognizable while describing certain situations.

In March 1985, coordinator Linda Bryan-Viliesis and I were listed in the newsletter *What's Up* as the joint winners of the winter-quarter director's award. Linda was nominated for her extra-mile efforts on behalf of the American Association for Colleges of Teacher Education–sponsored Commission on Excellence hearings, and I was nominated for "day-to-day excellence in handling a very detail-oriented job."

There is one funny incident that happened to me while working. Well, it's funny now, but wasn't at the time. Embarrassing would be the word that comes to mind. Back in the day, we used to wear pantyhose under our dresses or skirts when going to work. Those of us who tended to carry more weight than we liked chose not to add another layer by wearing panties when wearing pantyhose. It didn't seem necessary since the pantyhose were just that—panties—even though you could see through them. But since they were under your clothes, what did it matter, right?

One day I was wearing my favorite skirt and blouse and feeling all cute and darling. I usually ate lunch in the cafeteria in the Urban Life Building at Georgia State University. I worked in the building and it was convenient.

Before going into the cafeteria, I stopped by the bathroom as I usually did, then continued prancing through the cafeteria feeling all cheerful. I went through the line, taking my time to choose my food carefully with nice healthy vegetables and such, because I was usually watching calories. After picking my food, I stopped at the cashier to pay. The cashier leaned over and whispered to me, *"Ms. Thomas, you need to pull your skirt down. The hem is caught up in the waistband."* Oh woe, I had just pranced around the cafeteria exposing my backside to anyone who happened to look up from eating their food or anyone who happened to be in line behind me. The jerks could have told me, but I'm thinking they were enjoying my mishap far too much.

If I'd had a cute behind like, say, that exercising fool Jane Fonda or someone of the same caliber, I probably wouldn't have minded so much, but here I was with *my* posterior, such as it was, exposed to all the world—well, the cafeteria anyway!

After dislodging my skirt tail from my waist band, I could not have left the cafeteria soon enough nor could I have been more embarrassed than at that moment. The next stop at the bathroom would be to throw up!

While working as a conference coordinator, I did encounter a rather unstable coworker whom I'll refer to as Delusional Della, or just Della for short. Maybe I should have been flattered that someone found me so worthy of attention. I've still no idea why Della perceived me as either her twin or an enemy, but I suspect either jealousy or craziness played a part. Once she asked if she could borrow my GSU ID card because (she implied) we looked so much alike. I was not flattered, nor did I loan her my card. Not only was she overweight, but she was in no way professional in her daily attire. Let's just say she came up with some unusual outfits. That was one of the times that I was in possession of some unwanted weight myself, so maybe I should withhold judgment.

Again, I'm not quite sure why I was of such interest, but she seemed to focus on causing me problems—especially after my refusal of the ID loan. Her mode of operation was to be quite creative by either telling lies about me or inventing ways to sabotage me, which she did manage to do a time or two with management. What did they know, it was her word against mine. I believe the reason that nothing much ever came of her antics was that coworkers as well as management took her increasingly odd behavior into account.

One incident occurred due to the fact that a group of us often went to happy hour on Friday nights. At one such event, I dropped some items from my purse, and Della helped me pick them up. I thought nothing of it, until the next Monday, when she went to our supervisor with a receipt of mine claiming she'd found it in her office that morning. According to her, it must mean that I'd been snooping around in her office overnight. What? Why, I couldn't imagine, but again it was her word against mine, and the supervisor had no way of knowing it was a silly ruse.

On another occasion, she went to the director of the division reporting that I'd encouraged the group of coordinators *not* to buy a Christmas gift for our supervisor. The actual fact was that she had made the suggestion, and I'd just gone along with it. It didn't seem that important at the time. The outcome was that the director later called a meeting in which I was accused in front of the whole group, and I was too stunned to even deny it. Another incident of "she said, she denied," because I don't think the other coordinators considered the situation important enough to remember who had made the original suggestion. The only consequence was my short-term discomfort, which, I'm sure, was not nearly enough punishment to ensure Della a victory, but that's all she got. Was she trying to get me fired? I still have no idea what her intentions were or why.

After all this, I started getting hang-up phone calls at home. I endured the calls for several weeks before I called the phone company to get them stopped. AT&T asked that I record the dates and time of day of the calls. The phone company did get the phone calls stopped, but refused to tell me who had been doing the calling. Hmmm, I wonder to this day.

There were a couple of supervisors during my tenure who could have used some better management skills of their own. One of my methods of overcoming bad management was to apply for another job within the university system. My skills and evaluations were good enough that I was successful in doing that the few times it was needed. I mainly wanted to stay within the system because it offered good benefits and a good retirement package, which was a good decision when I retired.

The time came when the Division of Continuing Education had an upheaval or reorganization, and I opted to apply for a job at an off-campus site. Word had it that the director of that unit was difficult and employees didn't last long under his/her direction. Being an optimist, I didn't believe anyone could be that bad, thus my application and acceptance for that job. I got the job and was soon a believer in the rumors I'd heard. He/she was every bit as bad, or worse. So again I was seeking another job, and I moved back to the downtown campus, where I ended up working in the College of Law.

For the most part, the COL was a good move and a good experience. While working directly under Dean Marjorie Girth as I did when first there, my job was mostly arranging events for visiting dignitaries, both local and from abroad. Again, my organizational skills surely were helpful. These events included organizing all things required: hotels, locations for meetings, meal planning, hiring caterers, overseeing any printed materials, and basically whatever was needed for that particular event.

An example of one dignitary was the visit of Supreme Court Justice Sandra Day O'Connor. (See photo section.) An interesting aside is that US Marshals are hired to guard the justices, and I was surprised that her marshal was an attractive blonde woman who blended into those gathered around rather than standing out in a grey pinstriped suit with earpieces in her ears like the secret service. Since they're supposed to be unobtrusive, she worked well in that position.

While at the COL, I worked under several directors. Some were good, but one was, well, a horror, for lack of a better word. Okay, maybe "misogynist" is a better word. Anyway, it was a man whom I will refer to as Rooster (obviously not his name).

At first when I noticed that he took credit for the achievements of others, I didn't think too much of it. That sometimes happens. But when I noticed that he had a way of managing to have others blamed when he made mistakes, I became leery. I watched him do this on various occasions, so when he focused on me for a reason of which I'm still not sure, I was forced to defend myself. It involved both of us writing letters stating our cases to the dean. Eventually, I asked human resources to intervene by interviewing us both, and he refused. My question would be "If he had nothing to hide, why refuse?" If this had happened in the recent "Me Too" environment, it might fit as someone with power using the power inappropriately. Thank the good Lord his behavior toward me was not sexual, but it was harassment nevertheless. Fortunately the dean allowed me to be moved to the Career Services Office, where a very capable supervisor, Beth Brown, ruled the roost. Working with the very accomplished Beth is a fond memory.

For reasons not shared with me, Rooster soon decided to move to another city, and after all was said and done, I learned through rumor that he was a wife beater at home. With this information, I felt vindicated in my assessment of him. I was not surprised to learn this bit of information about his home life, but was glad that such activity would have been frowned upon in a work environment. Whew! Another of life's obstacles overcome!

Working in the Career Services Office turned out to be a good move for me. Eventually I was promoted to the title of program planner/analyst. My actual job was career counselor to law students. I advised them how to dress professionally, how to conduct themselves in interviews, how to write résumés, cover letters, and thank-you notes after interviews. For instance: never, never lie on a résumé, but there are ways to enhance the truth. With some students, I helped them find ways of overcoming unexpected obstacles in their job searches.

One such student I will refer to as Pollyanna, Anna for short. During the fall when law firms selected students to interview for associate jobs, Anna came into my office with a very worried look on her face. When I asked what was wrong, she explained that she had finished an interview that hadn't gone well. She said that she had been nervous, spilled papers, and basically described a disastrous interview. In trying to make her feel better, I said, "Well, that doesn't sound so awful, Anna." She said, "But then I threw up." I didn't say it out loud, but I was thinking, *Oh my Lord, how do I fix this?*

I decided the best way to tackle the situation was to be direct with her thank-you letter after the interview. I had her write something like the following:

Dear Mr. Smith,

Thank you for the interview, and I'm sure you will remember me. I am the one who threw up in your office. As it turns out, I had the flu and 103-degree temperature that day.
If you will still consider hiring me, I will do a good job for you and promise not to throw up in your office again.

Sincerely yours,

Pollyanna Jones

Sometimes a good excuse along with humor helps to overcome obstacles. I'm pleased to report that Anna got the job.

Toward the end of my time at GSU, having worked for twenty years at the university, things were getting more and more stressful in the work environment. As people left their jobs, money was tight, and rather than hire new people to fill the empty slots, it seemed that the workload was being spread among those workers already there. It didn't mean more money, just more work.

I was now working sometimes ten to twelve hours a day during the busy seasons of recruitment, sometimes more. My stress level became such that I decided my health was worth more than staying in a job that was no longer enjoyable, and I decided that it was time to retire. So that's exactly what I did.

Fortunately, I'd made many lasting friendships during the years while at Georgia State University that continue to this day. Working at a university, you meet interesting people and make wonderful friendships. (Photos included at the end of chapter sixteen.) One longtime friend I met there was Betty Henry Thom. Her cheerful nature brings lots of entertainment to my life. Betty has two sons: John Michael Thom, a businessman who has two sons (Scott and Connor) with wife, Vicky; and Laurence Thom, who is best known by his professional name in the entertainment world as Larry Tee. (See photo at end of chapter sixteen.) Due to his mother's cheerful personality, it's easy to see how Larry Tee was destined for the entertainment industry. A brief description of Larry Tee and his career is that he started in Atlanta, went to New York City, London, and is now based in Berlin. He is a DJ, club promoter, and music producer who coined the term electroclash and has helped launch the careers of such artists as RuPaul, Fischerspooner, Peaches, and Avenue D, to name a few. The most famous song that he composed is the one RuPaul made famous called "Supermodel (You Better Work)." In 2014 he launched his clothing line TZUJI at London Fashion Week. It is easy-wear, hipster sportswear worn by popular stars like Jimmy Fallon, Rihanna, Missy Elliott, and other hipsters. Needless to say, he gives Betty plenty to brag about when they talk via Skype from the various places he travels around the world. And I'm quite sure that I'm safe in saying that Betty is the only person ever driven to the hospital for heart surgery by co-team Larry Tee and RuPaul.

Many of my GSU friends are still in my life, and I don't dare try to mention them all for fear of forgetting some, but I must mention my friend Irene LaFleur, with whom I meet for lunch every week or two. I wouldn't miss getting together with her cheerful, positive personality that is a *pick-me-up* each and every time. I've included photos of some other GSU friends with whom I meet on a fairly regular basis and who will be named with the photos. (Irene's photo is included at the end of chapter sixteen.) Of course, there are some I don't see on a regular basis anymore, like talented artist Susan Coats. Susan has had at least three husbands since we retired from GSU, and I'm not going to try to remember all their last names, so I am just using her maiden name here.

I still love all my GSU friends, remember them fondly, and hope I haven't forgotten anyone whose name should be here.

*Working as coordinator at Georgia State University Continuing
Education Department*

*Nina coordinated Justice Sandra Day O'Connor's visit to Georgia State
University College of Law*

Justice Sandra Day O'Connor making speech during her visit to GSU COL

Chapter Nine
My Prides and Joys (Eric and Ethan)

Most parents and grandparents think that their children are the cutest, smartest, and most talented children on the planet, and I'm no exception. My son, Alexander Eric Thomas (Eric), has always been, what can I say, my pride and joy. No surprise here, I'm sure. He was a beautiful, sweet little boy. After he was grown, my friend Lois from Tucson days told me that she'd been afraid that he would be "too pretty" when he grew up. He is a nice-looking man, but more cute and manly than pretty. I think a nose injury from a diving accident into a swimming pool when he was in high school may have helped to "unpretty" him somewhat. So Lois's worry was for naught.

Don't we all wish we could have a "do-over"? In looking back at my life, I realize that I made mistakes and could have been a better human being. Starting out with a loving family in Appalachia certainly was a good beginning, and I feel blessed. Even with some of the challenges in life I've bragged of overcoming, I was blessed with a wonderful son and later an adorable grandson. I realize that I wasn't the perfect mother. Lord knows I tried, and to use an expression used in my family many times, "I did the best I knew how at the time." Hopefully most if not all my mistakes have either been forgotten or at least forgiven.

I can report that in his high school years, Eric was never without a girlfriend, and all were smart and pretty. If there was a breakup for whatever reason, there was hardly a pause until there was another girlfriend. And no, I never knew the reasons for breakups. Not that he would have told me if I'd dare ask, anyway.

As mentioned in the section about the trip to London (see the trips section) that Eric and I took together, Eric can be brave or tough if the situation calls for it, but he is also a caring and sensitive person. (Maybe I did something right!) After his "rock band" years, he got a job at his high school alma mater, the Paideia School, as a teacher and soccer coach. He is a terrific coach who has taken his team to the state championship four times now, but who's counting?

In addition to his accomplishments both as a soccer player and coach, he has competed in several kinds of races. He started out running in the 5K races with his dad, like the annual Peachtree Road Race in Atlanta. He branched out to running marathons, which is a feat beyond my comprehension. And then he competed in Ironman marathons, which just blows my mind, but I'm proud of all his accomplishments. What mama wouldn't be?

Much like his dad's past teaching experience, Eric goes above and beyond to help students and soccer players in any way he can. The Paideia School is a private school and not affordable for all, therefore they have an annual auction to raise funds to offer scholarships for students who can't afford the tuition. They strive to have a diverse student body, and some of the soccer players are from different backgrounds and/or countries.

One such example of Eric's sensitivity to his student players is as follows.

He knew that a particular student's mother did not speak English and would be unable to help him pay for or enroll in college when the time came. He not only helped the student get a scholarship to attend a college in a state several hundred miles away, but knowing the mother couldn't afford to get him there, Eric drove him. Each time the student needed to come home to visit his mother, he drove to get him and then take him back. He did this throughout the student's college career until he graduated. When the kid graduated, Eric (almost like a proud father) attended the graduation and later drove him to the state where he'd gotten a job. Eric would never tell all this and will probably be unhappy that I've told it, but it is the best way for me to explain what a kind person he is and how proud I am to relate just one incident of my son's thoughtfulness.

Along with his sensitivity and other good qualities, Eric is fun. He has the gift of gab, which means he can talk to anybody most anywhere. He gets that from his dad, and I envy that ability. He has a terrific sense of humor and can ad-lib on the spur of the moment. Another enviable trait. Just the other day his former mother-in-law, Coach, said that she misses him and his sense of humor. They still see each other on occasion, but not on a daily basis as in the past.

I'll always love Amy Hightower, if for no other reason than because she gave birth to my grandson. She was one of Eric's first relationships in high school that later grew into a significant relationship. He and Amy knew each other while in (different) high schools and dated. I have no idea where or how they met, but Eric tended to know kids from all sorts of different schools. Eric attended the Paideia School, and Amy attended Mount Carmel Christian School. Both went to college after high school graduation and went separate ways.

In the meantime, Eric had been in a rock band for a period of time and attended college, where he played soccer and graduated. Amy had gone to college, and gotten married and divorced. After all that, they saw each other at an art festival and started a relationship once again. The important fact about the relationship this time is that it produced my precious grandson, Ethan.

Amy's mother, Mary Ann Hightower (nicknamed Coach by her grandchildren), and I became good friends and remain so. Eric and Amy were together several years while raising Ethan. I was never confident that their relationship was necessarily a lasting one, but they're both good people and good parents. They have different parenting styles, but they seem to make it work. I fondly remember when they were together; sometimes they were secretive for whatever reason adult children tend to be. Coach and I just enjoyed a laugh between the two of us knowing that they were thinking they were sparing us either grief, disapproval, or worry. Those sweet, young things thought we didn't know what was going on. Kids tend to think of themselves as having more modern and superior knowledge and, thus, dismiss their "elders'" opinions—especially

when it comes to child rearing. Coach and I were confident that
they would eventually realize that with age comes wisdom worth
hearing and considering. We were confident of the fact that as they
age they'll face the karma that old age brings, but in the meantime,
it reminds me of the saying attributed to David Mamet: "Old age
and treachery will always beat youth and exuberance." Now
they've moved on as a couple no longer, but I can happily report
that we all still consider each other lovingly as family. Family gatherings now include an extended family of ex-spouses as well as the
original cast of characters.

We grandparents of Ethan all enjoyed taking turns keeping him
when he was a baby while his parents worked during the week.
Both Coach and I kept him on the days that surrounded the one day
that Granddaddy Bill kept him. Those are days that I cherish. Ethan
was such an alert baby and little boy. Even in diapers he noticed
pictures hanging on the walls and loved classical music. I'd heard
music was good for math skills, so I played it for him on occasion.
Lord knows I could have used it when I was in school, so I figured
I'd give him a heads-up.

His interests changed as he grew up, and I tried to entertain
those interests. There was a time he was interested in anything
Egyptian, pyramids and you name it; later he was interested in cars,
and we used to draw cars (interiors and exteriors). If I didn't draw
them to suit him, I'd have to draw until I got them right! Such fun!
We did literally hundreds if not thousands of car drawings. Later
his interests turned to architecture, and as it turned out, he is a naturally talented artist—so says his nana (me) and his art teacher at
school, Joe. Now that Ethan is a teenager, he has extracurricular activities, studies, and naturally friends who take precedence over
Nana, so I don't see him as often. But family gatherings work well
for now.

When Eric and Amy's relationship ended after several years, he
reconnected with a friend he once knew in high school. Laurie
Tharpe Beck came back into his life.

Eric and Laurie were both nearing middle age when they got

married in a sweet ceremony at the cottage they'd bought on a lake in Jackson, Georgia. The cottage is located in between where they both work. It is convenient because they're both teachers and each has about the same distance to drive to work. Their marriage seems to be a perfect match. Even after a year or more of marriage, they're still in the honeymoon stage. Eric, of course, has Ethan, and Laurie has two children, Lillie Claire and Hilton Beck. The blended family seems to be working well. The fact that I now have to manage a drive that takes over an hour to visit them is a pain in the posterior, but the fact that my son is in a happy marriage makes it worthwhile, so I'll adjust.

Since their marriage, we've all had get-togethers that have included all sorts of "blended families that included all our exes." This past Thanksgiving, Eric and Laurie hosted the dinner, with invitations to Eric's ex, Amy, and of course Ethan, myself, and my ex, Bill, and his wife, Jeanie, as well as Laurie's mom, Sue Tharpe, and of course Laurie's children, Lillie Claire and Hilton. I took a friend. It was a lovely festive occasion.

The next month, for Christmas, Amy reciprocated and invited Eric and Laurie and myself along with Bill and Jeanie for brunch and opening gifts. Amy's mom, "Coach," made her annual breakfast casserole, which we ate, and we exchanged some gifts there. From there, I went back to the lake cottage with Eric and Laurie to exchange gifts with them along with Sue, Lillie Claire, and Hilton.

Life seems to have worked out to be one big, happy, combined and extended family. Who woulda thunk!

L–R: Ethan's mother Amy Hightower and daddy Eric holding Ethan, Reverend/Dr. Jesse C. Walter Sr., who baptized baby Ethan. Ethan wore his great-grandfather Thomas's christening gown at his baptism.

Betty Thom and "Coach" Mary Ann Hightower, Ethan's Hightower grandmother

*Eric and his wife,
Laurie (Tharpe) Thomas*

*Eric and Laurie were
married by Eric's longtime
friend, (Judge) Matt
McCoyd, on the dock of
their lake house*

*Friends Matt McCoyd and
wife, Caroline L. Ahmann*

*Pure joy! Ethan and I used to make and decorate cakes on holidays.
This one was a Halloween confection!*

Eric and Ethan, showing Ethan growing taller than his dad

Love this photo of Eric and Ethan napping together

Young Eric (approx. age four)

Eric played soccer in high school and college

One of my favorite photos of Eric in high school

Favorite photo of Ethan and me, taken Thanksgiving at Eric and Laurie's lake house with all the blended families and exes in attendance

Grandson Ethan Alexander Thomas's school photo (2017)

Grandparent's Day at The Paideia School: (L–R) Ethan's granddaddy Bill, Ethan, grandmother (Nana) Nina, step-grandmother Jeannie, and grandmother ("Coach") Mary Ann Hightower

Chapter Ten
Appalachian Cuisine and Mama King's Recipes

I was excited about an article I read in the *Washington Post* (March 29, 2016) by Jane Black titled, "The next big thing in American regional cooking. Humble Appalachia." Yep, that's where I was born and raised for most of my youth—right smack dab in the middle of Appalachia in a town called Pennington Gap, Virginia. It is where the people I loved most lived all their lives, and some still do. As I've gained (and lost) weight over the years, most folks would not find it surprising that I have a fond relationship with food.

If "Appalachian cuisine" sounds like an oxymoron, get over it and adjust your thinking. One of the chefs discussed in the article is Travis Milton, and his restaurant in Bristol, Tennessee, is called Shovel and Pick. Being a girl from a coal-mining community, I love that name. He discusses the difficulty of finding ingredients that were used in the "old days."

The article also states, "Ask most people what they think Appalachian food is and their answer—if they have any idea at all—will probably be corn bread and pinto beans." That would be accurate up to a point, because those are two of the "comfort foods" I grew up eating, but there is much more to it.

My excitement is mostly due to the fact that I'll have a chance to talk about my maternal grandmother, Ruby Barlow King, whom I called Mama and whom I adored. (I called my mother just that, Mother.) Mama King was a terrific cook in what has now been designated Appalachian cuisine. Since Mother was divorced, my brother, Jack, and I lived in an extended family, the household of my maternal grandparents. That meant that Mother worked and Mama King was usually at home cooking three meals per day, and we often had others join us for meals. (See photo of Mama and her china cabinet and tea-making crock pitcher.)

Uncle Fred, Mama's only son, was a mail carrier, and he often dropped by for "dinner," meaning the noon meal. We referred to the three meals of the day as breakfast, dinner, and supper. I think that was the case in most of the South during the time when farmers worked long hours in the field and came home for a late "supper," which was sometimes after dark.

Meals were important to a family that enjoyed meals and comfort in each other's company. It was a mode of entertainment, especially on Sundays, when the immediate family was joined by others who might be visiting. The Sunday dinners consisted of Southern specialties, all home-cooked from scratch: meals could range from fried chicken to meatloaf, to pot roast, to chicken and dumplings, to turkey and dressing, and beyond. Vegetables were nearly always fresh, rarely canned, and could include green beans (half-runners were the type favored by my family); potatoes, prepared differently depending on the meat being served that day—potato salad, mashed potatoes, and home fries were some favorites—corn on the cob or creamed; and a mixture of greens that could consist of kale, mustard, beet, or other available greens, usually cooked together with fatback or a ham hock or a bit of bacon grease. If fatback (basically a small chunk of fatty bacon) wasn't available, there was always an old coffee can containing bacon grease nearby to use for seasoning. Modern cooks would probably use either butter, margarine, or vegetable oil, if anything at all other than salt and pepper, but fatback was the old-fashioned way. In winter, vegetables would be those that had been home-canned when they were fresh in the summer and stored in an underground cellar. Potatoes and other root vegetables were also stored in the cellar for use throughout the winter. Mama King was famous for her homemade desserts, which we always had on Sundays: pies (chocolate, butterscotch, apple, blackberry, or peach cobblers), boiled custard, cakes of all kinds (chocolate, applesauce cake, jam cake, yellow cake, or white cake), and banana pudding, to name a few.

Southerners are known for two basic breads, biscuits and corn bread, but Parker House–style yeast rolls (homemade by Mama occasionally on Sundays) were also a favorite of our family. And there is one more bread that I loved in my youth. It was "store-bought" salt-rising bread. I was delighted recently to find a bakery that still makes it, and I am able to order it. The bakery, Rising Creek Bakery and Café (in Mt. Morris, Pennsylvania), describes it this way: "Salt-rising bread is an old-fashioned bread originally made by pioneer women throughout Appalachia in the eighteenth and nineteenth centuries, before yeast was available. The bread develops its delicious cheese-like flavor from a unique fermentation process using wild microbes. [I've no idea what that means, but the bread is delicious!] The name is a misnomer, as there are only twenty milligrams salt in each slice. We think the name comes from a type of salt used in the fermentation." I can vouch for the fact that it would be hard to find a better sandwich than a grilled pimento-cheese sandwich on salt-rising bread.

Breakfast was the meal at which we had biscuits, usually along with sausage or bacon and eggs. Sometimes sausage gravy made with milk would be served with biscuits. I liked sorghum (syrup), a lighter version similar to molasses, on my buttered biscuits. (That would be real butter, never margarine.) Rhubarb jam was another favorite. My nephew, Chris, still maintains that Mama had a "magic pan" to produce those delicious biscuits. The noon meal, dinner, was when we had corn bread, along with the vegetables that quite often came in the form of pinto-bean soup (known to us as "soup beans") and coleslaw, or mac and cheese on occasion. The soup-beans-and-corn-bread combo is still one of my favorite comfort-food meals. Coleslaw was made with the sharpened end of a tin can that Mama used to chop the cabbage. The protective rim had been removed from the can, leaving the very sharp end open for chopping. A variety of foods were served on different days.

I make no claim to being a nutritionist, but I've read that the combination of the corn in corn bread and the pinto beans (containing protein) make up a very healthy combination. I think it was something like amino acids and protein, but whatever the combination, it is a healthy and inexpensive meal used by many Southerners, both those working in the fields and those lucky enough to eat in their kitchens.

In those days, folks ate only fresh food. It was so fresh that Granddaddy, who had been crippled in an auto accident years before, used his one good arm to wring the chicken's head off. The chicken would then flop around on the ground, for blood-letting I assume, before Mama plucked the bird clean of feathers and cleaned it. At the time I didn't associate all this with the delicious "fried thing" that ended up on the table later in the day. Or maybe I chose not to associate the two.

We were "pretty set in our ways," as the saying goes, when it came to food. In other words, we were particular. When it came to tomatoes, we only used heirloom tomatoes fresh from the vine. Heirloom vegetables are those grown from original seeds that have not been tampered with to make them perfectly shaped or colored as they are when bought in grocery stores. Even today, Thomas Jefferson's Monticello continues to sell (available online) heirloom seeds that were used in his garden. Think of it—eating tomatoes grown from seeds that graced Thomas Jefferson's table! Those tomatoes come in various shapes and colors, but the taste is far superior to any store-bought newer varieties.

For snacks or light meals, we enjoyed grilled pimento-cheese sandwiches, fried bologna sandwiches, or peanut-butter-and-banana sandwiches. Tomato sandwiches were on white bread with mayonnaise.

If my life sounds idyllic up to this point, I must add that it wasn't all white bread and mayonnaise—though I must say that mayonnaise did play a big part in my life, because you can't be Southern and not like mayonnaise. It's an unwritten law. Every Southern gathering has pimento-cheese sandwiches, which basically consist of grated cheddar cheese, pimentos, and mayonnaise. Nowadays, folks doctor up their pimento cheese by adding jalapeño peppers, grated onion, garlic, creamed cheese, or other ingredients that might strike their creative fancies. They're all good, and I always have a batch of the basic recipe in my fridge. The reason being that when Eric comes to visit, that's the first thing he does—heads for the fridge for the pimento cheese and some crackers.

Although we enjoyed spaghetti on occasion, we did not have food with fancy foreign names in French or Italian. I remember once when Mother brought home a box of Chef Boyardee pizza mix. I thought that was the most exotic food I'd ever eaten. As I remember, it consisted of a crust to spread on a baking sheet and tomato sauce to be topped with parmesan cheese and baked. Not until years after I left my hometown did they have fast-food restaurants like McDonald's, Hardee's, or Subway. As far as I know, there are still no so-called "fancy" restaurants there, but you can find some serving good ol' "Southern cooking."

At Christmas, one of Mama's gifts to her daughter (my Aunt Marilyn and her family, who lived in Cincinnati) was to mail either her jam cake, fruit cake, or applesauce cake.

My favorite was, well, anything chocolate. Below are some of Mama King's most-used and family favorite recipes that you might try and, hopefully, enjoy.

SOUP BEANS/PINTO-BEAN SOUP (A SOUTHERN STAPLE)

2 cups of pinto beans soaked overnight in 6 cups of water. Next day when ready to cook, pour off the soaking water and replace with fresh water. Use at least 6 cups (or more) of water. Mama King just used fatback (or bacon grease) to season her soup beans, with salt and pepper as needed. It is good her way. However, I've updated the original soup-bean recipe, and I add chopped onion, bell peppers, and a 14.5-oz can of chopped tomatoes. I add the onion and bell peppers at first, and then about halfway through cooking, I add the can of tomatoes. Sometimes I add a can of whole-kernel corn at the end of cooking as well. Spices added by me are (to taste) garlic powder, onion powder, and 1/2 tsp. crushed red pepper flakes, with

chili powder and salt and pepper as needed. You can be as creative as you like with this recipe, but try it this way first. If soaked overnight, the cooking time should be about 2 and 1/2 hours, and it should be stirred several times while cooking. Just check for doneness. Of course, corn bread is served with soup beans!

MAMA KING'S CHOCOLATE PIE

1 cup sugar, 1/4 cup cornstarch, 3 egg yolks, 1/4 cup cocoa, 1/4 tsp salt, 2 cups milk, 1 tsp vanilla. Mix all ingredients (except vanilla) and cook in a double boiler, whisking constantly until thickened. Remove from heat and stir in vanilla. Let cool slightly before pouring into a prebaked pie shell*. Then chill in the refrigerator. You can use the egg whites for meringue if desired, which means that you will beat the egg whites to stiff peaks, pour on top of the chocolate, and broil for a few minutes (watching carefully) until peaks are just lightly browned.

*Note: Mama made her pie crust, but I find it easier to use a store-bought crust these days.

This next recipe is one that was not initially Mama's, but one that she and the family adopted because we all loved it. I got the recipe from a former boss and friend named Jim Arnall. I worked for him at the University of Tennessee's *Daily Beacon* newspaper as an advertising artist. It is called Charles Corn Bread (I haven't seen Jim since we left Tennessee when Bill graduated, so there is no answer as to who Charles was).

CHARLES CORN BREAD

1 cup white self-rising cornmeal, 1/2 cup corn oil, 2 eggs, 1/2 tsp salt (optional), 1 cup cream-style corn (8.5-oz can), 1 cup sour cream. Mix all ingredients together and bake at 400 degrees for approximately 30 minutes in an *iron skillet*. (This recipe also makes 12 corn muffins that would take less cooking time, approximately 20 minutes.)

MAMA KING'S CHOCOLATE BUTTERMILK CAKE

2 cups flour, 1 tsp soda, 1 1/3 cups sugar, 1 cup buttermilk, 1/2 cup shortening (or oil), 2 eggs, 1/3 cup cocoa. Cream together shortening and sugar, add eggs one at a time. Add flour & milk alternately. Mix well. Bake at 350 degrees for 30–35 minutes (depending on oven). Test for doneness by using a toothpick inserted in center. Mama sometimes used either chocolate icing or caramel icing on her chocolate cake. Either choice was delicious.

HOECAKES
(SAVORY, CORN-BREAD PANCAKE-LIKE "CAKES")

1 cup self-rising White Lily cornmeal, 3 tbsp bacon grease (modern version would be 2–3 tbsp canola oil), 1/2 cup buttermilk*, 1 egg. Mix well. Heat an iron skillet with 1–2 tbsp oil and add hoecake mixture in 1/4-cup measures. Skillet will usually hold about 3 "cakes" at a time. Fry the hoecakes much like pancakes by watching for the bubbles to form on top, and then turn to the other side with a spatula to finish cooking. This recipe makes about 5–6 hoecakes.

*Note: If you don't have buttermilk on hand, you can use milk and add a few drops of either vinegar or lemon juice and stir to use as a substitute for buttermilk.

GREEN BEANS

Start with "a mess" of your favorite green beans. A "mess" to a Southerner means the amount you would use for a meal, probably about 2 lbs of beans that have been washed, strings removed (if needed), and snapped into bite-sized pieces. Mama snapped between each bean, but that's optional*. Cover beans with enough water to cover and parboil beans for 5–7 minutes. Then pour off that water and cover with fresh water to cover. Add salt, pepper, and approximately 1–2 tbsp of vegetable oil or butter (Mama would have used fatback or bacon grease) to cook beans until the doneness you prefer. I think probably 20 minutes would be about right for today's tastes, but check for your own preference.

*Note: Some green beans, such as pole beans, do not need to have strings removed.

CREAMED CORN

4 ears corn, 3⁄4 cup milk, salt and pepper to taste, 2 tbsp butter or margarine, 1 tsp cornstarch. In a skillet sprayed with cooking spray, cut corn kernels off cob and run knife down cob to mash out corn milk from cob. Mix in milk, salt and pepper, butter, and cornstarch and cook on medium heat for approximately 10 minutes. Mixture will thicken, but if it gets too thick, add a bit more milk for creamy consistency. Remove from heat and serve.

MEAT LOAF

2 lbs ground chuck, 1/3 cup chopped onion, 1/3 cup chopped bell pepper, 1 tsp garlic (or garlic powder to taste), salt and pepper to taste, 1⁄2 cup oatmeal (uncooked), 1 slightly beaten egg, 1 tbsp Worcestershire sauce, 1⁄4 cup ketchup*. Mix all together and place in a loaf pan. Top with more ketchup or BBQ sauce if desired, then bake at 350 degrees for approximately an hour. Pour off grease, slice, and serve.

*Note: You can substitute BBQ sauce for ketchup.

POTATO SALAD

2–3 lbs potatoes, peeled and diced into bite-sized pieces. Cover with cold, salted water and cook until just done (but not soft), approximately 15–20 minutes. Drain off water. In a bowl, add to potatoes more salt if needed to taste and pepper, 1 small (2 oz) jar diced pimentos (drain juice), 1/3 cup diced bread-and-butter pickles (or may substitute sweet pickle relish), 1/3 cup diced onion (or more if you're an onion lover), 4 diced hard-cooked eggs, 1/3 cup chopped bell pepper, and at least 1–1 1/2 cups mayonnaise. Add enough mayonnaise for a creamy mixture. Salad can be served right away or after being refrigerated. I've been known to add chopped parsley to this recipe, but Mama King did not*.

*Note: New potatoes (thin-skinned like yellow gold potatoes) are easiest to use because you can cook them whole and scrape skins off easily, then cut up into dices. You'll have to let cool enough to handle.

MAMA'S FROZEN SALAD

1 cup mayonnaise, 1 (8 oz) pkg softened room-temperature cream cheese, 1 cup (13 1/2–oz can) drained pineapple tidbits, 1 cup chopped nuts (either pecans or walnuts), 1 pkg lime Jell-O (dissolve as directed and chilled to semi-jellied but not solid state before adding fruit and nuts), 1 cup heavy cream or Cool Whip. Mix all ingredients into the semi-jellied Jell-O mixture. Place cupcake papers into cupcake pan and fill cups with the Jell-O mixture and freeze. When ready to serve, remove cupcake papers and place the individual-cup helpings on lettuce leaves to serve*. *Note: This recipe would not be used for an everyday-type meal, but on a special occasion or on Sunday.

MAMA'S SWEET ICED TEA

2 cups boiling water, 2 family-sized tea bags. Cover and steep for 15 minutes. While still hot, add 1 cup sugar and stir to dissolve. Add 6 cups of cold water. Serve over ice. Lemon slices optional. (See photo of Mama's crock pitcher that she used. Probably at least two hundred years old or more by now.)

MAMA'S APPLESAUCE CAKE

1 cup softened butter, 2 cups white sugar (less if applesauce is sweetened), 2 beaten eggs, 2 1/2 cups applesauce, 4 cups flour, 1 cup raisins (optional, more if you like them, but I changed recipe to use dried cranberries instead of raisins), 2 cups chopped nuts, 4 tsp soda, 1 tsp cinnamon, 1 tsp cloves, 1 tsp allspice, 1/2 tsp salt. Cream butter and sugar together, then add beaten eggs, soda, and applesauce. Mix well. Sift together flour, spices, and salt and add to sauce mixture, leaving enough out to flour the raisins and nuts (this keeps them from sinking to the bottom). Last, add the fruits and nuts and bake in tube pan in a slow oven at 300 degrees for 1 1/2 hours.

(EASY) PEAR SALAD
(SOMETIMES FOR SUNDAY DINNER)

On each individual salad plate, start with a lettuce leaf, top with half of a canned pear, add a dollop of mayonnaise on top of the pear, and then top with shredded cheddar cheese.

APPALACHIAN APPLE STACK CAKE

Although Mama made this cake on occasion, I don't have her recipe, but this cake has been used in Appalachian communities and families for generations, or at least it was. One article reads: "The hallmark of cooking in the Mountain South is resourcefulness, making utterly delicious dishes from modest ingredients." The stack cake is one such example. Thin layers of cake are sweetened with sorghum and filled with sauce made from dried apples. I'm sure there are many different family recipes to be found on the internet, but the following is a good one: www.ourstate.com/appalachian-apple-stack-cake/.

BANANA BREAD
(MOTHER-IN-LAW NAOMI VANLEAR
THOMAS'S RECIPE)

1 stick melted butter (or margarine), 1 cup sugar, 2 eggs, 2 cups self-rising flour, 3 ripe bananas. Mash bananas, mix all ingredients together, and pour into loaf pan. Cook at 350 degrees for approximately 40 minutes (depending on oven). Check for doneness with toothpick if need be.

My sweet Mama King

There aren't enough nice words in the English language to describe my Mama King or her cooking!

A painting (36" x 36") I did of Mama from a photo of her as a young woman

Cabinet built by Mama King's father, George Washington Barlow, my great-grandfather, and crock pitcher Mama K. used to make her sweet tea

Chapter Eleven
Jenny Lou and Nina's Great Summer Adventure, Destination: The Big Apple

I was always trying to find ways to entertain my widowed mother, Virginia King Stacy Wallen, who lived in a small town in Virginia. Since she had never been to New York City, one summer I decided it was high time she went. I figured you need to experience New York City, if at least once in your lifetime.

But let me start from the beginning of this mother-daughter adventure. First of all, Mother would not fly, so any plans must not involve airplanes. I lived and worked in Georgia. As I said, Mother lived in a small town on the southwestern Virginia border near where Kentucky, Tennessee, and Virginia meet.

This means that I had to travel the 350 or so miles to Pennington Gap, Virginia, to pick up Mother before we could even begin our trip. I also realized it would not be safe or reasonable for me to try to drive in New York City, which was another problem to be solved. So I did what every red-blooded American does these days—I got on the internet and explored Amtrak. Surprise, Amtrak does not have routes anywhere near Pennington Gap, so I decided that our best bet would be to drive to Washington, DC, and catch Amtrak from Union Station to New York's Penn Station. Travel time was approximately three hours.

An interesting aside is that in traveling on Amtrak from Washington to New York, we traveled through five states: Maryland, Delaware, Pennsylvania, New Jersey, and New York. Which means that, all told, counting Georgia, Tennessee, and Virginia, I traveled through eight states to get Mother to New York.

The only worry about the trip was that both of us had a variety of physical problems with which to deal. Mother, being in her eighties, had back problems, and I had a bum knee on which I eventually had surgery . . . but later. Regardless, we weren't going to let whatever ailments we had deter us from having a good vacation.

We embarked on our little trip with no particular plan except those dictated by the hotel reservations I'd made in Washington and New York, so the first night we stopped in Staunton, Virginia, and stayed in a nice little motel. I hadn't driven through my home state of Virginia in many years and had forgotten how beautiful it is. From Staunton, it was just a short trek to Washington the next day.

I'd made reservations at a hotel in Washington that was supposedly downtown. W-e-l-l, this phantom hotel could not be found. When I'd spoken with the reservation person on the phone, she said it was at 1600 New York Avenue, near the White House. Now, I don't know which "white house" she was referring to, but it was not the one at 1600 Pennsylvania Avenue. We finally found New York Avenue, but never did find the hotel. So, after I phoned the hotel to cancel our reservation, and had your basic tantrum—after which they assured me that a charge would not show up on my credit card—we found a really nice hotel, where (without reservations) we paid an arm and a leg to spend the night. All in all, though, we enjoyed our drive around Washington seeing the sights. It is a beautiful city.

The next morning we drove to Union Station, where we parked our car and caught the train headed for New York City. Ours was Train #174, "The Yankee Clipper." Isn't that cute? At the station, we had breakfast. We'd given our luggage to a "redcap" who met us after breakfast and guided us to the train. It'd been years since either Mother or I had been on a train, so it was almost like a new experience. They didn't have a dining car, but they had a car where you could buy snack-type foods. By that time I was in need of a "Diet Coke fix," big time. (Much to my chagrin, I found that some parts of Virginia must be Pepsi country, and Pepsi just doesn't do it for a Georgia girl—home to Coca-Cola.)

We arrived at Penn Station around midafternoon. The redcap

helped us locate the place where we could catch a cab, and of course, there was a line of folks already waiting. There in line we saw our first celebrity, the writer Kurt Vonnegut Jr., who was waiting for a cab along with the rest of us. No, I did not bother him, though I was tempted.

Now comes one of many New York cab-driver stories, all of which are true. They all seem to be of foreign extraction and rude, not that one thing has to do with the other, because I think rudeness is just inherent in cabbies. On the first cab ride, the driver insisted that the Hilton Hotel on Forty-Second Street and Broadway at Eighth, where I'd made reservations, did not exist and refused to take us there. Finally, I told him to take me to the DoubleTree, which is where I'd called first and discovered they were booked, at which point they referred me to the Hilton. Normally, I would have insisted that he take us, but after my experience in Washington, I wasn't that certain myself. At the DoubleTree, the concierge called to confirm my reservation at the Hilton and explained that this was a new Hilton that had just opened two weeks ago on Times Square. Is that a good location or what?

We caught another cab headed to our destination. When we got there, he was trying to get into a parking space across the street from the hotel. As he was attempting to park, a construction worker in a truck started yelling obscenities at the cabbie, and the cabbie started yelling obscenities back. After this went on for a few minutes, I told Mother to get out of the cab and we'd manage to get across the street on our own. After we paid, the cabbie took off peeling rubber, and the construction worker in the truck peeled rubber while getting into the much-sought-after parking space. It was a New York moment for Mother to witness.

Since we were only staying two nights, we splurged on the hotel and found it worth it. Our very expensive room was wonderful. There was a terrific view of part of the Manhattan skyline and the river. We overlooked Forty-Second Street. We enjoyed a really nice dinner at the hotel with the best wine I'd ever tasted and a piano bar.

I knew that neither of us could walk long distances and decided the best way for Mother to see New York would be a double-decker bus tour the next morning. After the tour, we caught a cab to Greenwich Village, where we ate at a charming little café. The weather was blazing hot and we were tired from the bit of walking in the Village, so we headed back to our good old air-conditioned hotel room before going to see a play that evening.

Since I didn't have one of my favorite New York things at lunch, I decided that Mother and I needed to head to the famous Carnegie Deli for dinner before going to see *Chicago* that evening. The deli is another New York experience everyone must have. The two guys seated next to us were having these huge sandwiches. I asked what they were and was told they were having the "Woody Allen sandwich" (what else?), which is a mixture of corned beef and pastrami. I opted for just the corned beef, which was served with a bowl of kosher pickles. Delicious.

We went to see the play *Chicago* (long before the movie came out) starring, among others, Sharon Lawrence, Belle Callaway, and Brent Barrett. It was wonderful, and Mother made my day when she looked over at me during the play and said, "This is worth the whole trip."

We took the train back to Washington the next morning and decided to drive a bit before stopping for the night. As we passed signs to Lexington, Virginia, Mother asked if that wasn't where my cousin Jane lived. It was, and we called meaning just to say hello, but as I should have known any Southern girl would do, cousin Jane insisted that we spend the night with her and husband Bob.

To say that they were gracious would be putting it mildly, because they were doing renovations on their house and certainly didn't need company. So, the next day before leaving, we took them out to eat and say farewells.

When we arrived back to Pennington Gap, we were tired but happy travelers. I was happy to be home. I still faced the trip from Pennington Gap to Georgia the next day, but with fond memories of a trip that Mother and I enjoyed together.

New York trip with Mother
Mother relaxing in the robe supplied by the Hilton on Times Square,
where we stayed

Chapter Twelve
Trip to London with Eric

Briefly, another trip I instigated was a trip to London with my son, Eric. I saw a good deal for a trip to London and had some vacation time available, so I called Eric and said, "How would you like to accompany me to London? I'll pay." His response was, "Sure." Since this was a spur-of-the-moment decision, I got on the computer to do some research, where I found good accommodations for us when we arrived. It was November, which is probably why there was a good deal—weather in London not being the best "visit weather."

I won't go into a lot of detail about this trip, except to say that we managed to hit most of the "hot spots" of London. I don't drink coffee. Not because I don't approve, but because I don't like it. Eric, however, is a coffee addict, or maybe a better word would be connoisseur. That meant we discovered many Starbucks or other "like cafés" throughout the trip.

Just before landing in London, the flight attendant announced that a passenger had an announcement to make. I was thinking, *Oh no, a hijack!* But no, thankfully, it was a marriage proposal, which was sweet, and everyone clapped and cheered.

We found the British very friendly and helpful. I was already having some physical ailments with knees that made lots of walking difficult for me, but that would become apparent much later in my life. For now, I could manage. Eric, however, was a regular at going to the gym, so he immediately found a gym where he could work out while I adjusted to the time change and stayed in bed in the mornings. He became quite a fan of the Tube, while I loved the taxis for transportation.

We compromised, and he rode with me in taxis to most other events (and some from a tour bus). And yes, we saw lots of sights:

the changing of the guard at Buckingham Palace, the Crown Jewels at the Tower of London, Madame Tussauds (for fun), Piccadilly Circus, Covent Garden, Trafalgar Square, the National Gallery, the Houses of Parliament, Westminster Abby, 10 Downing Street, the Tate Gallery. I went to Harrods for lots of gift shopping (because everybody knows that name), but my favorite department store was Selfridges. I'd often go there for tea while Eric continued to explore some place he wanted to investigate.

One incident worth mentioning happened while Eric and I were walking one night in an alleyway-type street that they refer to as mews. I don't remember where we were headed, but we saw three young men walking toward us, and we both had that unspoken sixth sense that says they could mean trouble. Without a word, Eric immediately moved to the side that would put him in between where I would pass the young men. As it turned out, a car came over a small hill behind the young men that gave them pause, and no incident happened. Of course, I've no idea what would have happened, but there was that sixth sense that something could and probably would have.

Though it has nothing to do with the report of our London trip, I must add my pride in my son. He played soccer from a young age through school and college. He was an aggressive soccer player who played in the state championship in high school and now coaches soccer teams at the Paideia School, where he graduated. The teams he coaches have also won several state championships. I say all this because Eric can be aggressive when the case calls for it, but he is also a sensitive and caring human being. I have no doubt that he would have protected me if the case called for it in the mews. He would do the same for anyone in need of it, and has on numerous occasions.

On another occasion while in London, both Eric and I forgot that it was my birthday on November 30, but when it finally dawned on us, we went to a nice Italian restaurant for dinner. It was our most expensive meal of the trip, but hey, it was a celebration! All in all it was a fun trip for me and my grown-up baby boy.

Eric and beefeater

Harrod's, of course

*The Tower of London
(and they didn't lock us up!)*

Chapter Thirteen
Early-Marriage Trip to California

A lot of the road trips I've taken, if not most, have been with my ex-husband, Bill, and all were an adventure of one sort or the other and remembered fondly. At the time I was not as impressed with them as I am in looking back. Geez, we were brave and adventurous back in the day—if not just plain stupid at times. We rarely had enough money to embark on said adventures, yet we managed to achieve our goals and live to tell the tale.

We had very little money in our pockets when we decided to drive to California from Knoxville, Tennessee, where we were living at the time. Since we had little money, Bill thought it would be a good idea to drive straight through without stopping. Yes, from Tennessee to California. First, can you believe he suggested that? And second, can you believe I agreed to it? Well, I did use the word stupid earlier when I should have said "young and stupid." Regardless, that was the mindset on which we started the trip.

Stupid me thought I could do that, but somewhere along the way, I was so tired that I started crying and begging him to stop at a motel for rest. Here's the sad scenario about the car: it was an old Austin-Healey that didn't have a heater and had to be pushed off to start. Bill finally found a really cheap motel (we're talking Bates Motel here) and stopped. In an effort not to freeze to death, I had on several layers of clothes with a hoodie on top. When we got to the room, I didn't even undress before going to bed. Did I mention there was a blizzard going on outside? It seemed like I'd just gotten to sleep when Bill woke me saying we had to leave. There was a shutter that kept banging on the window. It sounded like something from the movie *Psycho*, a movie that had left a scar on his psyche years ago. He couldn't sleep and insisted on leaving.

It was the middle of the night and the blizzard was in full force.

Since I wasn't able to push the car off to get it started, Bill saw a bar across the street where a man was coming out and whom Bill asked to help get us pushed off. The man suggested that I get into his big ol' warm car—a Buick, I think—to get warm while he helped Bill. (No, I wouldn't think of doing that in today's world!) He was pushing Bill off with his car, and there I sat inside this strange man's car. It had beer cans and liquor bottles covering the floor, and I did have the sense to be scared enough to keep my hand on the door handle until I could safely get out. I don't know why I was worried, because if you remember my description of myself, I certainly couldn't have been an object of desire in layers of clothes with a hoodie on top, not to mention sleep-deprived and wearing no makeup. The poor good samaritan was probably more scared of me than I of him—either that or he was drunk enough not to care. Regardless, the man helped, and we were on our way once again. Believe it or not, we made it to our destination unscathed.

This was the trip where we started our married life together and where we ultimately had our precious baby, Eric, in a hospital in Oceanside, California. We briefly stayed with my dad and his family in Escondido before we found an apartment in the little town of Vista. While in Vista, Bill's sister, Mary, came to live with us and attended Palomar College.

Dad's wife, Cynthia, worked for the San Diego County Social Services Department and helped Bill get a job there as a social worker.

Photo of Nina taken by Bill at the Grand Canyon

Chapter Fourteen
The Trip through Texas

When driving through Texas, you tend to think that you'll never get through the state, but eventually you manage.

On one memorable and amusing trip, we had stopped at a shopping center and were on a side street waiting for a light to get back onto the highway. While we waited, a car came up behind us and bumped into our bumper. It wasn't a huge bump, but the driver didn't get out to check, which upset Bill. When Bill got out to check, so did the driver in the other car, a distinguished, older man with white hair. It was before cell phones, so when a bystander offered to call the police, we all agreed.

The older guy asked if he could drive his grandchildren home before the cops arrived; we agreed after taking his information. The older guy left before the police arrived. When the cop arrived, he was just what one would expect of a Texas cop: Stetson hat, cowboy boots, and all of six feet tall. The cop was taking our statement when the old guy came back. When the cop looked up and saw the old guy, he said, "Oh, hello, Your Honor." Well, well, well. Bill and I just looked at each other and didn't say it, but thought, *Oops!* In fairness, the cop did give the old judge a ticket, but whether he ever paid it would be up for debate.

Chapter Fifteen
Last Big Trip with Bill—
A Memorable Adventure!

Any trip I ever took with my ex-husband, Bill, turned into an event of one sort or other, especially interesting when looking back. In the words of writer Nora Ephron, "Even bad experiences are fodder for writing." To me, they can be looked at as a hurdle that was either enjoyed or overcome.

Bill and I lived in Atlanta, and the ultimate destination for the road trip I'm about to describe was San Francisco for a political science convention (for Bill's work), but with plans of visiting friends and sightseeing along the way.

We drove to Tucson, Arizona, where Bill had gone to the University of Arizona to finish his doctorate before we moved to Atlanta. We still had friends in Tucson, one of whom was Lois Putzier. Our first stop was to pick up Lois for a side trip to Mexico, which was Lois's favorite place to go when she was between husbands. She joined Bill, me, and our son, Eric, as we headed for San Carlos, Mexico. The first night we ate in a nice restaurant, where ten-year-old Eric ordered chicken that came to the table on a flaming sword. Needless to say, this started his vacation with excitement. Ah, but there was more excitement to come.

One afternoon, Lois and I went into a beachside bar after swimming. While there, a gorgeous blonde (American) male approached, introduced himself, and sat down. As mentioned, Lois was between husbands, so I'm sure she was drooling. I was trying to figure out how to handle the situation if he pulled the ol' "just happen to have a friend who can join us" line. However, being married did not keep me from noticing the clearest blue eyes, blondest hair, and most golden tanned skin I'd seen in a while. It didn't help

that he was wearing a Harry Belafonte–type shirt open to the navel
. . . though, mind you, I wasn't *really* paying much attention. My
ego was a tad deflated when it turned out that the handsome hunk
was trying to sell beachfront condominiums rather than hitting on
us. I was surprised and relieved when Lois didn't pretend to be interested in buying a condo.

We enjoyed the many activities that San Carlos had to offer, but
on the last day there, we were in for a shock. We decided to take
one last dip in the motel pool. Bill was walking on the beach, while
Lois, Eric, and I played Marco Polo in the pool. I looked over to see
Lois floating facedown in the water and, thinking she was playing
a prank, gave her a gentle tap on the back. When she didn't rise
from the water, I realized it was serious, and in a panic, started
screaming. What else? Fortunately, we were in a nice motel where
many well-to-do Mexicans vacation. Which is to say, they speak
English, but I'm sure screaming doesn't need much translation.
Several men ran to help get Lois out of the pool. They tried CPR,
and it didn't seem to be working. They did finally get her breathing,
but she was unconscious. Those bystanders who seemed to be "in
the know" suggested that we take her to a private clinic rather than
a hospital. Actually, the police rather demanded that we take her to
the clinic called Sanatorio de Sanchez, owned by one Dr. Sanchez. I
rode with Lois in the most terrifying ambulance ride one can imagine to the clinic. Bill and Eric followed in our car.

Once at the clinic, we knew we couldn't leave her there. Let's
just say it didn't look as sanitary as an American clinic. But mainly,
we wanted to get her back to a Tucson hospital where she had in-
surance. Dr. Sanchez suggested we air-ambulance her to Tucson, so
we agreed. Well, surprise, surprise, Sanchez not only owned the
air-ambulance service, but I discovered the next morning that he
was also the pilot. I was elected to fly back with Sanchez and the
still-unconscious Lois while Bill and Eric drove back in the car.

After seeing the clinic, I didn't know what to expect of the air-
plane in which we would be flying. It actually looked okay, but I'm
no judge. It was painted, had propellers and a motor, and thus

passed my unqualified inspection. I'll admit to still being a bit shaky from the whole ordeal plus worry about Lois. Sanchez's nurse rode with us but spoke no English, and what little Spanish I'd had totally left my brain. We managed to land in Tucson, where Lois's friend and boss, Gary Buck, met us with the 9,447 pesos ($750) that Sanchez had insisted on immediately after landing. From there, I'm thinking he and the nurse went on a little vacation, but that's just my speculation.

Bill, Eric, and I were forced to leave Lois in good hands at the Tucson hospital while we continued our trip to San Francisco in order to make it to the political science conference. Of course, we checked with Lois's friend, Gary, frequently about her progress.

Dr. Sanchez's diagnosis had been that of a water accident, which was not a bad diagnosis considering the circumstances, but the doctors in Tucson found that she had a brain aneurysm, which was successfully operated on, and she recovered fully.

Lois Putzier died in 2013 from lung disease. But after the 1975 water accident in Mexico, she lived an active life for thirty-eight more years. Lois was an activist for many causes that she felt strongly about. She and her next and last husband, Jerry, used to visit me each November. Their main reason for the visit was to protest the School of the Americas at Fort Benning, Georgia. The School of the Americas, as I understood it, was training Latin American soldiers for combat. The protest was about human rights abuse in the Latin countries when the soldiers returned. At Fort Benning, the protesters were not to cross a certain line while protesting or they would be arrested. Well, Lois did just that, got arrested, and spent some time in prison. It was a real prison, mind you. I don't remember the period of time, but it was enough to get her attention and remind her not to do it again. When she became disabled with the lung disease that eventually took her life, she was no longer able to make the November trips, but we maintained contact throughout her life.

On the remainder of that trip, we visited with friends along the way that included Phil and Linda Simpson in Lawton, Oklahoma.

Next we visited the Painted Desert, the Petrified Forest, and the Grand Canyon. The San Diego Zoo, I'm convinced, has to be the most beautiful setting for a zoo. Of course, we had to make a visit to Disneyland for Eric, where he and Bill took off like jets and I just tried to keep up. Some of the most beautiful scenery in the USA is along the California coast where the University of Santa Barbara is located and continuing up the coast where Big Sur, the Monterey Peninsula, Pebble Beach, and Carmel are located. Yep, we managed to do all this and enjoyed a meal at the John Steinbeck Lobster House on Cannery Row on our way to the political science convention in San Francisco.

After leaving San Francisco on the way back home, we stopped in Salt Lake City and visited the Mormon Temple Square. We were amused that ten-year-old Eric wanted to visit the Coors brewery in Golden, Colorado, before we left that state. That was before Coors was accessible east of the Mississippi River.

Chapter Sixteen

Old Age and
Activities after Retirement

Realizing you're old comes as a shock, because it seems to happen suddenly! You start noticing crow's-feet around the eyes one day, while on another day you see more wrinkles showing up, and later—the worst—crepe-paper skin emerges. Oh woe! All those expensive creams and lotions don't work anymore, if they ever did!

It is no secret that old age brings with it all the aches and pains. I had knee-replacement surgery, and much later I was forced to have back surgery. Not forced by a person, but from the pain that I'd fought for years that kept getting progressively worse. I put up a valiant fight before doing it. I tried acupuncture, chiropractic treatments, and shots to my back. But alas, surgery became necessary.

Now, I'm not going to get morbid here, so just bear with me for a minute, then I'll move on to fun stuff. Sadness comes as you start losing folks close to you. I've already lost a lot of family members, and even some friends. My mother lived to be ninety-five years old. I like to think she had a nice, long life knowing how loved she was by all who knew her and certainly by me. Her death is a grief I'll never get over. My one major regret is that I may have caused hurt for the one person who never let me down in all my life. She was so ill that she had to be hospitalized toward the end. I was exhausted from caring for her 24/7, so when hospice could take her from the hospital to a hospice facility for a few days before I brought her home, I was relieved. My thinking was that I could use some rest, and they could set up hospice home-care furniture while she was at the facility. My friend Coach (Ethan's other grandmother) and I went to see her after she was settled at the really nice hospice facility that afternoon. My usually sweet, loving mother was angry. I kept trying to explain to her that this was temporary and she'd be coming home as soon as her room was set up for her return to it. She kept saying, "I don't believe you." When she was finally sedated enough to go to sleep, Coach and I left around 9:00 p.m. At 11:00 p.m., hospice called to tell me that my precious mother had died. I will never overcome my sadness that not only did she die alone, but probably thought I'd abandoned her at that facility. My heart has ached every day since.

One thing is for sure at this stage of life: it is lonely at times, so you have to find ways to entertain yourself. What does one do as a now-described "senior citizen"? Life forces you to either "get on with it" or let it defeat you. Since defeat isn't in my vocabulary, I get on with it. Of course, I look forward to any time I can spend with Eric and Ethan and family members associated with them, but they have their lives to live, so time with them becomes limited to when they're off work or school. I have to stay active, both in mind and body, as much as possible. I fill my time with painting pictures and, currently, writing this memoir. I have an art degree from Georgia State University, so why waste that talent? Attending workshops of interest is a fun adventure. I go to movies and to lunch or dinner with friends, or alone if or when necessary. Staying active is important!

For several years, I enjoyed being part of a trivia team that we named "The Mimosa Gang." We mostly played at The Corner Pub one night a week and often won. The team was made up of different genders and different ages, which I'm convinced helped us win. The younger members knew lots of pop culture that we older ones did not know. Unless it was a question related to art, I wasn't much help, but I enjoyed the night out with a group of smart friends. The guys were more familiar with sports. Our friend Laura Shannon, who I'm convinced has a brain like an encyclopedia, was the one we could always count on for the questions no one else knew. If she didn't know the answer, she could reason it out. Fun times fondly remembered. I've enclosed a photo of our little team.

As for painting, I recently entered three paintings, hoping to be entered into a juried exhibit at the ART Station Gallery in Stone Mountain, Georgia. I was pleased that all three were accepted into the show.

Some interesting workshops I've recently attended were writing workshops, where you meet smart, interesting, and talented people. Attendees are all different, which makes them each interesting in their own way. The last workshop I attended was taught by author Jim Auchmutey (*The Class of '65*) and former *Atlanta Journal-Constitution* newspaper journalist. From that workshop fellow student, Tom Matte, has since written an article ("Head Case," January 28, 2018) for the AJC and has a forthcoming book titled *Jesus Goes to Hollywood*. I'm convinced it will be a best seller once published. I'm sure others from that class will eventually be published in some form as well. (See photos of WS group and Writers Studio open house with authors.)

That class was taught at the Decatur Writers Studio. Later, I attended an open house there and was thrilled to meet more talented and published writers associated with them: Joshilyn Jackson (author of at least eight best-selling books that include *Gods in Alabama*, *The Opposite of Everyone*, and *The Almost Sisters*), Jessica Handler (author of *Invisible Sisters*), and Suzanne Van Atten (former Personal Journeys editor for the AJC), to name a few. I figure it can't hurt to associate with talented folks, stay active, and keep my brain cells challenged and working.

Another outing that I enjoy tremendously is the annual AJC Decatur Book Festival, the largest independent book festival in the country, with literally hundreds of authors coming to discuss and sell their books. Author Daren Wang (*The Hidden Light of Northern Fires*) is the founding executive director of that festival. I first heard him speak at the AJC book festival, where he shared the stage with Charles Frazier (author of *Cold Mountain*). Later, I had the opportunity to meet and hear him discuss his book at the Eagle Eye Bookshop (in Decatur) and found him to be as interesting (and charming) as his book. No doubt there will be more books in his future to look forward to.

Oh, and Facebook keeps me entertained and in touch with friends and relatives, many of whom live in different states. It entertains me to see photos of them, their children and grandchildren, and events they attend. And I like posting recent photos of Eric, Ethan, their accomplishments, and whatever it is that I'm doing at the time. Some of my high school friends and I stay in touch via emails, phone calls, and Facebook. For those who refuse to use Facebook, emails and phone calls work for those. I like Facebook when I'm feeling lonely or don't want to go out. It is a nice way to feel connected to the world and be entertained.

I'm fond of a statement attributed to the artist Georgia O'Keeffe, and it is one that describes my life:

"I've been absolutely terrified every moment of my life—and I've never let it keep me from doing a single thing I wanted to do."

Indeed, I have felt abandoned, lonely, and intimidated, not to mention terrified at times, but like O'Keeffe, I've always figured the way to overcome it would be to stay positive and associate with positive people. That would mean remembering and cherishing memories of the life I've lived, the hurdles I've jumped, and those yet to come. And especially remembering the good, loving family from which I came lo those many years ago, way back in Appalachia.

This is the Writer's Studio class taught by author of Class of '65 Jim Auchmutey. Jim is shown in the background and I'm second from right. I don't remember the names of all in the class, but all were interesting and talented writers, as was evidenced in each class. (Photographed by Pam Auchmutey.)

Nina and writing workshop classmates Kalin Thomas and Shellie Sims Welch at the Decatur Writer's Workshop open-house afterparty

Group of blended family at Eric and Laurie's lake house (including exes and friends). From L–R around the table: Bill, Eric, Laurie, Amy, George, and Larry. Others not shown in this photo.

The Mimosa Gang trivia team at the Corner Pub
(L–R): Liz O'Brien, Nina, Laura Shannon, Joey Lee, Moe Miller, and Matt O'Brien

My Georgia State University friends and I often met for lunch at Café Lily. Here on the left are Patricia Sartain, Susan Goodroe, Janice Arson, Sally Hilton. On the right are Jack Sartain, Nina Thomas, Carol Hollahan, Frances Stone.

Irene LaFleur and Steve Strickland, seated. Standing: Susan Goodroe, Sally and Bob Hilton.

A favorite: Pastries A Go Go, my Cheers restaurant, where everybody knows my name (and I know theirs). Owner Bob with some of his cheerful staff: "Cat," Amy, and Jenny.

My friend Latonia Jones, who works at CVS and who patiently helps me in making photo books and other technical things.

Pam Auchmutey, Nina, and author Jim Auchmutey attending open house at Decatur Writer's Studio

Writer Tom Matte, Nina, and Tom's wife, Christie, attending open house at DWS

Nina with author Joshilyn Jackson, a New York Times *bestselling author of eight or more books, including* Gods in Alabama *and* Almost Sisters *(attending Decatur Writer's Studio open house)*

Longtime GSU friend Betty Thom shown with her son Lawrence Thom, a DJ, music composer, and promoter professionally known as "Larry Tee." (See more about them in the Thanks and Afterthoughts section in back of book.)

Acknowledgments, Thanks, and Afterthoughts

Other than family, there are many friends, neighbors, and loved ones to mention, remember, and thank. So, here goes:

I must not forget my longtime neighbor friends. Some have moved away from the neighborhood, and others farther away . . . and some are still on the street. Sadly, some have passed away. But let's start with those still living, who were and are still loved and important to me: Jean and Ed Ellis, Liz and Matt O'Brien, Cathy and Luron McDaniel, Nan Franklin, Claire and Eugene Hertzler (Claire is the author of the book *The High Sheriff of Green*), Larry Cooper, and Debby and Moe Miller. I want to especially thank Debby Miller for being a listening block and editor while I labored to write this memoir. Also, I anxiously await the publication of her book, which will be titled *The Wayback Letters*. Thanks to all the others who have listened to me complain about the difficulty of writing a book, which was also helpful—and all encouraged me.

As for those neighbor friends who have passed away, they're still remembered fondly. Joan and Jerry Perkins were eventually divorced before they passed away, but they left many interesting memories as a couple. Jerry was a colleague of Bill's at GSU. Joan later married another of my very much alive GSU friends, Bartow Cowden. Bartow keeps me entertained on Facebook. Charlie and Kathryn Dodd lived next door for many years before their deaths. Adorable Charlie went first, and I think Kathryn never got over his loss.

Others who are still alive moved to other parts of the country or world. Eileen and Randy Guynes were another GSU friendship and were neighbors for a time. Randy was a colleague of Bill's in the political science department at GSU. Their son, Greg, and Eric were school friends who played soccer together. Will and Alice Berry (both professors) were a couple who had an adorable daughter, Vanessa (before they divorced), whom I remember as a little girl. She is now grown with children of her own and lives in Paris with her French husband. I've enjoyed connecting with grown-up Vanessa on Facebook, though I have not met her as an adult, but from photos, she grew into a lovely woman. It's weird the things one remembers, like, if memory serves me (and it doesn't always these days), I remember her mother's dissertation was on Gustave Flaubert. I had no idea who that was at the time, but I have since read *Madame Bovary*.

Since I mentioned some former neighbors who were also friends, I must at least mention some new neighbors whom I've had the pleasure of meeting more recently. They include Heddy Kuhl and husband, Steve Franklin (and children), who own the coffee shop JavaVino. After she discovered that I don't drink coffee, Heddy invited me to join her for a delightful tea one day—with fine china, no less. Doug Walker and wife, Catherine Such (and their four-legged "children," Linus and Ross), live across the street, and Doug was kind enough to gather my mail while I was gone one long weekend. Marnie Grodzin came to visit me often and brought treats and flowers after my back surgery. How sweet is that? Derrik and Jane Peavy and daughter, Elizabeth, are also new friends and a welcome addition to the neighborhood. And I have a neighbor friend who secretly brings my recycle bin from the curb to my back porch each week after trash pickup. I've never been able to identify who does it so that I can thank them, but I love the mystery of it.

Certainly worth mention is my longtime friend June Brown, whom I met while our sons (Eric and Jay) attended the Paideia School and played soccer together. June, our friend Blanche Thompson (who is now deceased), and I attended many soccer games, shopping sprees, meals, and bitching sessions together. (After all their shopping, June and Blanche once opened a [now closed] vintage shop called Half Moon Street.) June is a scientist who loved her job at CDC for about fifty years. Yes, I said fifty years. Who does that? Well, someone who loves their job and is very good at it. She is a microbiologist and the cowriter (with Michael M. McNeil) of an historical scientific paper entitled "The Medically Important Aerobic Actinomycetes: Epidemiology and Microbiology." Yeah, I have no idea what that means either, but as I understand it, a paper called "historical" in the scientific world means that it was read and referenced by scientists all over the world. Impresses the heck out of me too. Congratulations to my smart friend. June and I don't see each other on a regular basis, but when we do get together, it's as though no time has passed. We just pick up where we left off last time.

Thanks to Dick and Hanna Cortner for visiting with me on their trip from Arizona headed for an eastern vacation. We shared a meal or two together and visited the Jimmy Carter Center. I enjoyed their friendship while living in Arizona, when Dick was Bill's major professor and Hanna was a doctoral student and friend. It's hard to say how many academic books Dick wrote, but I remember him as a prolific writer. I love the fact that we're still in contact whenever possible. I think they mainly enjoy their retirement by traveling all over the world.

Thanks to my ex, Bill Thomas, for finally finding time (I'm sure he dreaded it) to come read the parts of this memoir that included him. I can't remember verbatim, but his comment after reading it was something like "It is more fair than I deserve." Now, admittedly, he later changed his mind and asked that a couple of things about him be removed, which I did—begrudgingly so, but I did.

Thank you to the team at BookLogix, who helped me through the ordeal of getting a book published.

It would be impossible to individually name all my relatives and lifelong friends, especially those from Pennington Gap. Some are still there and some have moved away. All of them are loved and worthy of mention, so I can only hope they know who they are and will be understanding if I have failed them in any way in this endeavor. This memoir is a love letter to them all.

About the Author

Nina Stacy Thomas is retired from Georgia State University, where her final move up the ladder was in the College of Law Career Services Office. There she advised law students on how to write résumés, cover letters, and other helpful bits of advice on the interview process. She was editor of the Career Services newsletter as well.

She lives in Decatur, Georgia (an Atlanta suburb), where she continues to remain as active as possible. Her favorite activity is spending time with her son and grandson, but when that isn't possible, she stays active with her painting and newest endeavor of writing by attending workshops, along with lunches and dinners with friends.

Recently she entered three paintings in a juried show at the ART Station Gallery in Stone Mountain, Georgia, and all three were accepted into the show.

In this memoir, she writes about her love of her family, friends, and hometown, Pennington Gap, Virginia, and Appalachia in general. Most importantly, she includes some of life's challenges encountered and how she overcame them.